SUBHAS ANANDAN

IT'S EASY TO CRY

Marshall Cavendish
Editions

Published by Marshall Cavendish Editions
An imprint of Marshall Cavendish International
1 New Industrial Road, Singapore 536196

Interview excerpts and tributes from the October 2014 edition of *Al-Mizan*, Vol. 1 No. 3 are reproduced with the kind permission of the Association of Muslim Lawyers. Special thanks to Mohd Mahdi Marican, 22, who conducted the interview with Subhas Anandan in the presence of Ms Fatima Musa, the co-editor of *Al-Mizan*.

Reprinted 2016

Other Marshall Cavendish Offices:
Marshall Cavendish Corporation. 99 White Plains Road, Tarrytown NY 10591-9001, USA • Marshall Cavendish International (Thailand) Co Ltd. 253 Asoke, 12th Flr, Sukhumvit 21 Road, Klongtoey Nua, Wattana, Bangkok 10110, Thailand • Marshall Cavendish (Malaysia) Sdn Bhd, Times Subang, Lot 46, Subang Hi-Tech Industrial Park, Batu Tiga, 40000 Shah Alam, Selangor Darul Ehsan, Malaysia

Marshall Cavendish is a trademark of Times Publishing Limited

National Library Board Singapore Cataloguing in Publication Data
Anandan, Subhas, 1947-2015, author.
Subhas Anandan : it's easy to cry. – Singapore : Marshall Cavendish Editions, [2015]
pages cm

ISBN : 978-981-4561-52-5 (paperback)

Anandan, Subhas, 1947-2015. 2. Lawyers – Singapore – Biography.
3. Trials – Singapore. I. Title.

KPP11.A53
340.092 -- dc23   OCN918510029

Printed in Singapore by Markono Print Media Pte Ltd

To all my siblings to whom I owe so much.
I know that this dedication is nothing compared to how you stood by me.

To my elder sister, Subhashini, who has been there for me in more ways
than one that I have lost count.

To my younger brother, Sudheesh, who is always there for me.
Silently strong, he gives me the confidence and the assurance to attempt
the things I otherwise would not have tried.

To my younger sister, Sugadha, who assures me of spiritual support.
Her prayers give me confidence to do the work I do.

To my beloved youngest sibling, my late brother, Surash,
who was my best friend. He encouraged me to do whatever I desired
and I really miss him very much.

CONTENTS

ACKNOWLEDGEMENTS

It has been six years since I wrote my first book *The Best I Could*. A lot has happened in those six long years, both good and bad. I have had the pleasure of working with friends and colleagues in KhattarWong LLP and then of helping set up RHT Law Taylor Wessing LLP.

My son, Sujesh, has decided to read law, a switch he made from banking and finance. Whether he chooses to practise criminal law is entirely up to him as I have always emphasised to him that he should pursue his own dreams.

My wife, Vimi, has been my pillar of strength through all the crises I have faced. She has always stood firmly by me, unwaveringly, constantly encouraging me and providing me with her love, kindness and understanding. She has been my soulmate ever since I first met her.

My legal practice has been my passion but I must say that the law was not my original choice of career path. I had thought of many other careers before I embarked on law. I was unsure as to whether I would practise law upon graduation but circumstances led me to commence practice after I was called to the Bar on 20 January 1971.

My health took a turn for the worse days after I launched *The Best I Could* in December 2008 but God was kind and I was back at work by early 2009, still chasing my passion in practice, especially pro bono work which I have been involved with since I started practice in 1971. This time, in addition to pro bono work, I visited schools and gave talks to encourage students and provided monetary support to students in need as much as I could. I have always been an advocate of a second chance and I believe that every one deserves it, if the need arises.

My health deteriorated further as evident in the increase in the number of pills I was taking a day but that did not deter my spirit to live life to the fullest. Knowing that Vimi and Sujesh were very understanding and supportive of what I do, I delved into anything and everything where I thought I could be of help to anyone, whether it was emotionally, legally or financially.

I have always felt that some of Singapore's criminal laws were ready for change, especially the right to counsel by an accused person on his arrest. I am also against the mandatory death penalty. I have always believed that the discretion of the hearing judge to decide on death penalty is most important but the law unfortunately binds the hands of the judge in such cases.

I have been honoured to sit on many steering committees in recent years. These include the committee set up by the former Attorney-General Sundaresh Menon, our present Chief Justice, to reform areas of criminal law and the committee set up by the Ministry of Law to review homicide. We have yet to settle on many of the proposed changes but I am glad that at least the process of formal discussion has started.

My dear friend, Noor Mohamed Marican, informed me one day that the Muslim Lawyers Association would like to organise a tribute in my honour. As I have always been very passionate about providing support for ex-inmates, he wanted to arrange a bursary award in my name with the Yellow Ribbon Foundation. Personally, I felt that this honour was too great to accept and told him not to pursue it. However, Marican, being Marican, would listen only to himself and did what he felt was honourable and befitting as I was already in the twilight of my practice. On hindsight, I thank him for it. It was truly an honour.

I have been on dialysis since the beginning of 2014 and it has been very hard to bear. It took a toll on me emotionally but in time, and with the support of my wife, I have learnt to keep myself occupied during the agonisingly painful four-hour sessions, three times a week. This was when I decided to dictate this book, *It's Easy to Cry*, which I had promised the publishers that I would do. It may seem disjointed as I would dictate as I sat in the dialysis chair and my thoughts would be different each day.

Subhas Anandan
December 2014

The launch of *The Best I Could* at Books Kinokuniya, December 2008.

FOREWORD

My beloved darling husband, Subhas. What can I say about him that has not already candidly been said by him and those who knew and loved him? He was my soulmate in every sense of the word. We have very different personalities but we connected at every level, be it about food, movies, gossip, serious topics of discussion, a joke or his work and passion to help those in need. He was ever willing to share with me everything in his thoughts.

Every day, I would pick him up from work. The moment he got into the car, I would ask, "How was your day?" That would spark a continuous monologue of his day in the 15-minute drive home. He never failed to share his day's experiences with me. Sometimes I wonder if he just needed me to ask him how his day was, so that he could just rattle on, not expecting me to grasp any of it. But I did and there were moments when he would seek my layperson's view on some matters.

I have known Subhas for two-thirds of my lifetime. We shared a great life together, through good and bad times, and came out closer and stronger for it. We share a son, a great person with a lot of his father's qualities and I can't ask for more. I admired Subhas' generosity towards others, his passion for helping the needy and his dedication to his work. It was totally fine for Sujesh and me to take a back seat when it came to his passion for work. He always knew we would understand and he made it a point to keep us abreast of his comings and goings.

Despite his busy schedule, Subhas never missed dinner at home with the family. He was a great father, who was first a friend to our son. He never failed to attend to our needs in any way he could. We knew that he put us above all else deep within him and we allowed him to pursue his passion, most of the time without troubling him. He appreciated this from us.

Subhas was also a very loving son and brother. His parents and siblings meant the world to him and he would do anything for them.

I will always treasure the memories that have been created between us and I will live the rest of my days appreciating and fondly reminiscing the love and joy he gave me.

With all my love,
Vimi

SUBHAS
ANANDAN

PREFACE

I was wrongfully detained in remand prison from the end of January to the middle of November 1976. While in prison, I toyed with the idea of writing a book about my experiences in prison. It was even reported in the press as I had mentioned it to a journalist on my release from prison.

David Marshall, who was my lawyer then, rang me up and told me, "Be careful, my lad. You don't want to look for trouble. You may state issues that are protected by the Official Secrets Act. I suggest that you hold on." I took his advice and held on for a very long time until 2008, when I decided to write my first book *The Best I Could*, which, to my surprise, became an instant hit. I initially thought to entitle it "It's Easy To Cry", but somehow when I wrote that book, I felt "The Best I Could" was more apt.

In my first book, I wrote of gruesome murders and some of the more unusual cases that I thought would be of interest to the reader. Many people think that crime means killing, lust, sex and money but this is not always the case. Sometimes, a commission of crime shows the true nature of a man or woman, and such a commission can be a noble act to save someone. Many of the cases that are mentioned in my second book depict situations where deep and complex emotions are displayed, like a mother who lies and pleads guilty to save her son.

So now, having the opportunity to write another book, I feel that it would be most appropriate to entitle it "It's Easy to Cry", because it is dedicated to cases that bring humanity and emotions to the forefront and to show that sometimes accused persons commit crimes of passion which they regret doing. This book shows to the reader that there are cases where people have pleaded guilty just to protect someone they cared for or to ensure that their loved one does not get into trouble.

In my new book, I also share my thoughts of people who have touched me one way or other.

Vimi felt that I should not write this book, as I was unwell, and especially when I was in the dialysis centre because I would get too emotional. When she heard the first part of my recording, she was convinced that I was indeed getting too emotional. I told her that it *is* an emotional book and I have to tell the story the way I want to. If it is emotional and if the stories arouse conflicting emotions in the reader, then I have succeeded.

ONE

GETTING TIRED

In August 2013, I was beginning to feel unwell, but I kept working. I was in my office when my assistant, Diana Ngiam, brought one of the submissions that she had prepared.

I looked at the submissions and said that there were missing points. She had failed to mention some of the facts that happened in court. She said, "You know, Uncle, I've gone through the notes very carefully." Then I said, "Go and look at it once more." She went back to her room and later realised that I was right. She approached my nephew, Sunil, who was also working with me, and said, "Uncle may be getting older but he is still very sharp. His memory is so good." Sunil laughed. She came back with the amended submissions, and this time I said, "Yes, this is what I wanted."

Diana is a very intelligent girl, very compassionate to all, including the accused persons. Sometimes she feels too much and that is not good, but I am glad that she's part of my team. After reading the submissions and approving it, I told her, "Diana, I've got a funny feeling that I will not be accompanying you and Sunil to court anymore. I somehow feel that my career is going to be over soon." She looked at me and said, "You may be a little under the weather but you are not going to die. Don't talk like that." She was very upset. I said that there was no point being upset for this was what I felt. She came closer and looked at me and said, "No, Uncle, you are going to be with us for many more years." I laughed.

The following month, I fell gravely ill and was taken to hospital. I was diagnosed with heart failure but after a few days' rest in hospital, I was discharged. Soon after, I resumed work but realised that I was not able to cope with a full load. I was in and out of hospital over the next couple of months, and fell ill again in the middle of December 2013.

Doctors were at their wits' end as to what they could do for me and several propositions were put to me, all of which I had initially rejected. One of the doctors gently explained to Vimi, and Chechy (my elder sister, Subhashini, as I address her in Malayalam) that my sole kidney was failing and there was nothing more they could do other than recommend dialysis, and even that was risky due to my failing heart. They offered palliative support if my family so needed it and indirectly suggested that there was nothing more they could do for me. On hearing this, both Vimi and Chechy decided that they were not giving up on me and with their faith in God, they believed that I would be well again. Vimi explained the circumstances to me and insisted that I should fight on. Gently, I told her, "Ask Dr Ching to see me." Associate Professor Ching Chi Keong is my cardiac electrophysiologist, who had recommended the insertion of a Cardiac Resynchronization Therapy Device (CRTD), which I had initially rejected. As it was the least invasive, I finally decided that I should give it a shot. I should not go without putting up a fight.

The procedure was a success but sadly, by then, my kidney had been impaired. I was required to go for dialysis three times a week. This altered my lifestyle significantly. I found it hard to cope emotionally and I would get upset with myself, depressed and frustrated with what I had to deal with — three sessions a week, being pricked twice on the

This photo was taken on 24 December 2013 on the eve of Subhas' 66th birthday. He was already listed on the 'Dangerously Ill List' and could receive visitors without restriction. Clockwise: Vimi, Sunita, Subhas, Chechy, Sudheesh, Syon, Sujesh, Sugadha, Sunil and Sharon (Sunil's wife).

arm at each session and being confined to an uncomfortable chair for four hours to dialyse my blood. It was during the long and weary four hours that I decided I should start dictating this book to keep myself occupied. It was very difficult to cope with the change and accept the fact that this situation would probably be my new way of life. In this depressed state of mind, I found it hard to get started writing this book. I would dwell on the past, remembering the times I could do so much and that would send me spiralling down emotionally. I would suddenly break down and cry uncontrollably, especially when I met with old friends who would reminisce about the good times we shared. It was certainly not their intention to upset me. They thought that reminiscing about the good times would cheer me up but instead I ended up feeling depressed as I knew that those days were long gone.

Once I am in that frame of mind, it was difficult to get out of it. It was so tragic. I would pray to God to take me away.

"Dear God, please take me away. I don't want to live anymore if I have to go on dialysis. It is painful and depressing and I am always tired and miserable."

Vimi and Sujesh have been solid support for me. Sujesh is studying in Nottingham but he would make every effort to return home to be with me. He told his mother when she asked if he missed holidaying with his friends, "All these places will always be there, but my father will not."

My siblings, Chechy, Sudheesh, Sugadha; my sisters-in-law, Syon, Justina, Nan, Komi and Lilian; my brothers-in-law, Nala, Nara and Bhas; nephews, Sunil, Suresh and Naresh; and nieces, Sunita, Seeta and Shona, were constantly by my side, not only supporting me but being a source of comfort for my wife and son. They took turns to visit me and encouraged me. Their presence and moral support opened my eyes to why I should fight to live. I tend to lapse into depression and each time someone would talk me out of it and show me life in a positive light. It has been an emotionally and physically tormenting experience coping with my poor health. I was previously racing through life, but suddenly, that lifestyle has come to a grinding halt. It was hard to bear. The positive thoughts that got me through these low points were my wish to see my son graduate; see my niece, Sunita, get married; and attend my nephew, Naresh's, wedding. Inevitably, there were moments of depression when I forgot these desires and allowed myself to dwell on negative thoughts.

Vimi would always tell me, "Be brave, think of positive things. Just know that your glass is half full and not half empty. We are here with you and I will never leave you. We will always take care of you.

Don't be afraid to fight this fight." Sometimes when I am down, I feel like no one understands me. I don't know why but I feel insecure and afraid that Vimi would leave me although deep within me, I know she will always be with me. When I am alone in my room or alone attempting to read a book, negative depressing thoughts would creep into my mind and that whole day is ruined.

It has been a very trying time for all of us but I must say that I am definitely feeling better and slowly accepting my condition and new way of life.

On some dialysis days, I get visits from dear friends like Ann (Vimi's best friend), Choo Poh Leong and Julia (friends from my teenage years), or Ah Teng and Ramli (my childhood friends). They always encourage and cheer

Subhas with his siblings on his birthday, December 2006. From left: Chechy, Sugadha and Sudheesh.

me up. I truly appreciate their visits. With the help of constant medical discussions and assurances of good doctors like Professor Ong Biauw Chi, Associate Professor Ching Chi Keong, Dr Manish Kaushik together with Chechy, my brothers-in-law, Dr A Nalachandran and Dr Bhaskaran K Nair, I have begun coping better with dialysis. I have settled into a routine that allows me to go back to office on days that I don't have to go for dialysis as my heart is getting stronger with the help of the CRTD. I have found myself in the right frame of mind to start this book and dictate whenever I can.

They say that in any incident, there will always be a silver lining. To me, my illness has made me a more realistic person, one who realises that in the past, I got all my priorities wrong. It was my career first, my career second, and my career third. I didn't make time for my wife and son. I didn't make time for my siblings and I didn't make time for my other relatives and very close friends. These are the people who are now with me through my difficult times. My sister-in-law, Komi, her husband, Nara, and their three children, gave me so much

With dear friend Choo Poh Leong.

moral support and encouragement through this difficult time. I feel quite blessed that I have people like them with me. Of course, my other sister-in-law, Nan, her husband, Nala, and their family, were always there for me, too. As is often with expectations, it doesn't surprise me that they are there, but sometimes you also wonder why some are not. It really doesn't matter. It is in the time of crises that you know who your friends truly are.

TWO

THE PASSING OF DEAR FRIENDS

After I wrote *The Best I Could*, many events happened in my life, one of which was the loss of many a dear friend.

"Botak Maniam", also endearingly called "Tata" (grandfather in Tamil), was the only grandfather that I knew who was young at heart and had so much compassion for his friends.

We first met at Naval Base School where we were studying. I was in the primary level and he was in the secondary level. He was then House Captain and a great sprinter. I admired his athletic abilities. Later he joined the Naval Base Police Force and retired as an officer.

It is somewhat strange that despite our age difference, we got along so well. He was a man of few words, always like an older brother to me, and incredibly dependable. We enjoyed each other's company and as we got older, we often indulged in card games, especially poker which he loved to play.

In his twilight years, he became seriously ill and was warded at Singapore General Hospital. Regrettably, I was told that I should not visit him as my immunity level was low from a recent illness. I felt miserable and anxious. Knowing that my dear friend Botak Maniam was so sick and I was unable to visit him, made me feel helpless with despair. Some time after that, one of our friends rang me and said that he was coming by to pick me up. He told me that Botak Maniam had passed away and he was taking me to his wake as the funeral was scheduled for the next day. I was all shaken up and despite being ill myself, I decided that I had to go especially if someone was making the effort to take me there.

When we arrived at Botak Maniam's home, I saw my dear friend lying in the coffin, looking so peaceful. I stood beside the coffin for a long while. His son, who was aware of my health condition, brought a chair and insisted that I sat down. I looked at Botak Maniam and thought, "This is going to be hard. I will miss you dearly." Unable to hold back any longer, I burst into tears. Friends who were near by, and who knew of my relationship with him, held my hand and assured me that he was finally at peace.

I couldn't take my eyes off Botak Maniam because seeing him brought back so many fond memories. I thought about the happy carefree days we shared with other friends in the Base and how we had grown old together. All I could do was just stare at him and think to myself then, "He was greater than anyone I ever knew." I will miss him forever.

Another dear and true friend whom I lost soon after that was Anthony Heng. He was someone I had mentioned in my earlier book. Sadly, he had cancer of the throat, like his father and brother. He suffered slowly and terribly and finally, he lost his voice.

By the time I visited him with Vimi at Tan Tock Seng Hospital, he was already unable to speak. However, that didn't dampen his spirits. He was very pleased to see us and greeted us with a broad smile. The memory of that smile is still lodged in my mind and it is a wonderful memory of a loving and caring friend whom I could always turn to for help. He held my hand for a long time and was deep in thought. I could see that he wanted to say so much to me. Then he took a notebook and wrote to my wife, "Look after him well and don't worry about anything. I will be waiting for him in the next world because, wherever he is, I will be there and I will take care of him." Vimi looked at him with glazed eyes and said, "I wish you well. I know that you are Subhas's dear good friend and that you will do whatever you can for him." I looked at him, unable to believe that Anthony was leaving us.

We visited him a few more times. Each time, he would hold my hand and look at me contentedly as though comforted by my presence. My being there was enough for him. Each time, I would hold back my tears until I reached the car when I would break down and cry. Vimi would console me and on one occasion, she said, "I understand how much he means to you. But you have to let him go." I replied, "No one will understand how good a friend he has been, unless you have been in prison with him."

KS Rajah was a State Counsel, Judicial Commissioner and, most importantly, he was my friend and fellow Senior Consultant at Harry Elias Partnership from 2000 to 2007. His room was next to mine and quite often, we found ourselves chatting and lunching together. There were times when he liked to argue on the law of criminal jurisprudence. I found that his arguments sometimes were not applicable to today's context but would be applicable in time to come. He was a farsighted man with old ideas, some of which were never respected. However, I always considered them with the greatest of respect.

We used to spend a lot of time with former Judicial Commissioner Amarjit Singh, who was then a Senior Consultant with KhattarWong. We would go for lunch and enjoy many spirited discussions on the law.

KS Rajah fell ill and when he was dying in hospital, he asked to see me. I went with my nephew, Sunil, and saw his family there. When he heard my voice, he sat up and said, "Ah, I am so glad you are here." I said, "I tried to come earlier but security did not let me in," and he laughed. He told his family, "You know, there's something about this guy. He always makes me think. Whenever I talk to him, he makes me think." Everybody laughed. Then he turned to his son, Suressh, who is a good friend of mine and a partner of Harry Elias Partnership, and said, "Look here, you are not interested in criminal law and neither is anybody in our family. So all my criminal law books, put them in a box and give it to Subhas. I bequeath them to him because I know he will make good use of them." I was so touched and almost broke down in tears. He asked me to sit by his side and held my hand. Squeezing it as tightly as he could, he said softly to me, "Look after your health. You are not healthy yourself, you know." In a near breaking voice, I assured him, "Yes, I will."

As I walked out of the room with Sunil, my eyes welled up with tears. All I could think of was how I came to know this great man and now he was leaving us soon, but I was glad that I had the last few moments with him.

In this book, I am sharing with you all my feelings very candidly about what I have gone through and practically baring my soul. Through these crises, I have learnt to cope with life better and face my greatest fears instead of rolling over and playing dead. I have this desire to fight to live, not for myself, but for my wife, my son, siblings and all others who are also dear to me. I am not ready to go. Today I am not worrying about what is going to happen tomorrow because I am not even sure whether there will be a tomorrow.

THREE

A CARING TEACHER

The first case worthy of mention is Public Prosecutor vs Shanti d/o Krishnansamy, involving a teacher who was charged for amending some of her students' answers in the Primary School Leaving Examination (PSLE).

Shanti was charged and pleaded guilty to three charges, punishable under section 468 of the Penal Code. Those offences took place on 5 October 2007. The presiding examiner of the school had erroneously appointed her to be the invigilator for her own class. It had never been the practice for the teacher of the class to invigilate his or her own students.

I give special mention to this case as it shows that there is no compassion at times from the prosecution. This teacher was asked to invigilate her own students. She saw some of the mistakes they made in an important life-defining exam. She was so shocked because some of the mistakes were so simple that she decided to amend them herself without realising the gravity of her actions. Not being in a right frame of mind at the time, she used her own blue pen and did not even try to copy the handwriting of her students. All she thought of was to rectify the simple, glaring errors.

Of course, she was found out because there was no attempt made to hide the fact that she had altered some of the answers. When she was caught and questioned by the authorities, she admitted very frankly that she had altered the answers. She added that she was very remorseful, and that she did not know what had gotten into her when she did it.

The simple fact that escaped the prosecution is that the Ministry of Education (MOE) mandates the invigilation of national exams by teachers who have no motivation to affect the result and who have no ties to the students sitting for the exams. It was clear that this was a one-off offence and that it was the result of an extremely unfortunate sequence of events. There was certainly no prevalence of such offences, no syndicate involved, no difficulty in detection as she had used her own blue ink pen and there was no public disquiet. Not many persons were affected and Singapore's educational reputation was not affected in any way. There was also no fear of such an offence recurring. Even if there was a probability of the event recurring, the public would have faith in our system that such an offence would be discovered and dealt with expeditiously.

To understand the teacher's mental framework, we must look back at her character, her achievements and her circumstances. Prior to this incident and the realisation of her mental disorder, she had been considered one of the better teachers in the school and had even received an award for being an efficient teacher.

She and her husband had been trying very hard to conceive a baby for a long time but were unsuccessful initially. There were a couple of miscarriages at the start and finally after ten years of marriage, in July 2000, she managed to conceive. She gave birth to a daughter but tragically her child had leukemia. This news completely shattered her as she had been looking forward so much to being a good mother. Fortunately, by 2003, her daughter was in remission from the dreaded disease. Although her mood and anxiety improved, she remained concerned about her daughter's health, which was natural for a mother whose child had suffered such a disease. Sadly, in 2007, Shanti's daughter fell ill again and Shanti was devastated. She was not allowed to take leave as she was in charge of the Primary Six Tamil Language students. In her opinion, she had acted her very best and despite her domestic situation, she gave her all to the students. She was so dedicated that she even felt like she had adopted all the students as her own. She did what she did with good intention and care.

When we were briefed to act for her, we had to take over the case from another lawyer. Soon after, we sent her to a psychiatrist, Dr Stephen Phang of the Institute of Mental Health (IMH). Dr Phang confirmed the assessment of private psychiatrist Dr Tommy Tan, that Shanti was suffering from depression. (Dr Tan said that Shanti suffered from chronic adjustment disorder with mixed anxiety and depressed mood. Dr Phang said that Shanti suffered from major depressive disorder.) This meant that there were occasions when she did not know what she was doing. Such a medical report would normally be sufficient for defence counsel to make a representation to the Attorney-General. In most cases, there was a chance that the charge could be withdrawn against the accused person or probation would be suggested as long as the accused person underwent medical treatment.

So with great hope, we wrote to the Attorney-General explaining the whole situation and stressed the IMH psychiatrist's concurrence with the diagnosis of major depressive disorder. Much to our surprise, we received a letter from the Attorney-General's Chambers stating that they were not acceding to our representation. They were going to proceed with the charge and were intending to ask for a custodial sentence of 18 months. We were totally shocked.

When the Deputy Public Prosecutor (DPP) arrived in court, I realised that he was once an intern in my office. I remembered him as a pleasant and helpful person during his internship period. He had shown much compassion for the clients who were in trouble. Now that he was in the Attorney-General's Chambers, there was a change in him. His demeanour was all tough and unsympathetic. I said to him, "What's happening, Ramu? This is really not fair, asking for this woman to go to jail." He replied, "Well, it's something that I cannot help you with because this is an instruction from my bosses." I could understand that he was just a messenger, coming to court to convey the wishes of his bosses. But I didn't like the way he said it, with a smirk on his face and without any trace of personal sympathy. When I said to my assistants "This guy has changed a lot," one of them replied, "What do you expect? He is now under the influence of other people, not you." Anyway, our client did not plead guilty.

We approached the Senior DPP who then told us the problem they were facing. The MOE was taking this matter very seriously and they wanted her to be punished. I told the Senior DPP, "I can understand the fact that they want her to be punished, but 18 months? That is really ridiculous, isn't it?" Even the hearing judge, Ms May Mesenas, was surprised at this demand. She called us into her Chambers and said that she was not going to give 18 months, but she also said that as it was a serious charge, she would not give probation. Then we went to open court. The prosecution wanted a custodial sentence of up to six months. We argued that a custodial sentence of one month or three to six weeks was sufficient. Subsequently, the accused was sentenced to two months in prison. She was released within weeks for good behaviour.

Shanti visited me at my office with her husband after her release. They thanked me for my help. I said to her husband, "I am so sorry that my assistants and I were not able to help her more." They said they could understand. She left the teaching profession and is now giving private tuition at home.

This is a case where many other factors were involved that should have been taken into consideration but were not. It shows that sometimes people commit acts which appear on the surface to be very serious but when you analyse the offence and the person who committed the offence, you will find that it is not as deplorable as the prosecution makes it out to be. I was very disappointed with the attitude taken by the Attorney-General's Chambers in punishing this woman who was actually mentally ill.

Just because the prosecution wanted to please somebody, they have forgotten the main principle of law and that is, fairness. You must be fair, even if you are a prosecutor. More so, you must show compassion. You must exercise your prosecutional discretion carefully. Sometimes, when it is necessary, you can exercise discretion in favour of the accused person. This would only go to show compassion and would not make you appear small and petty in the eyes of the defence. It would make you look noble and the defence counsel will say, "This DPP, he's tough but he is compassionate." But I suppose those values are not important to some DPPs or even to some senior DPPs.

FOUR

A MOTHER'S UNCONDITIONAL LOVE

I once helped a lady, Teo Sew Eng, who was the mistress of a very rich man. Unfortunately, the man was cruel and ill-treated her a lot, and she had to undergo psychiatric treatment for Dysthymia (persistent mild depression). He refused to divorce his wife to marry Teo even though she bore him a son. And although he had promised to give her $300,000 in the event of his death or during his lifetime, this promise was not fulfilled. He passed away when Teo's son was a teenager.

Before his death, Teo had identified him to her son as his father and shared her disappointment with the way he treated them. She also disclosed to her son where his relatives lived and the car that belonged to his paternal uncle. What subsequently happened was that her son, along with his friend, set fire to the uncle's car. The fire spread and a few other cars were burnt in the process. Unfortunately, the son had asked his mother to get the things needed for the burning, covering up his intention by telling her that he was having a barbeque with his friends. She had immediately got the charcoal and other required items and gave them to him. Subsequently, when the investigation proved that the fire had been deliberately set, the police arrested the son and his friend. His friend was sentenced to probation. We fought very hard for the son, who was the main culprit, and also managed to get him on probation but with restricted terms.

One of the things about probation is, if a probationer commits a new offence, he can be taken back to court and be punished for the original offence along with the new one.

In the meantime, Teo was charged for abetting her son in setting the cars on fire. She defended herself, saying, "No, I did not know that he was going to burn the cars. I thought he was going to have a barbeque." But when her son was arrested, he made a statement implicating his mother. He claimed that he did it because he was frightened and did not know what he was saying.

Anyway, the case against Teo went on trial. While her son was giving evidence for the prosecution, the DPP tried to impeach him on the basis that what he was saying in court — that his mother was not involved — was contrary to what he had stated to the police. Teo, who was sitting behind me, realised that her son was going to be in trouble. He would either be charged for perjury in court or he would be charged for giving a false statement to the police. Whichever way you look at it, her son would be committing an offence. She was afraid that his probation might be revoked and he would be sent to jail. As she was signalling and trying to communicate with me, she caught the judge's attention. He told me, "Mr Anandan, I think your client wants to say something to you." I turned around and she anxiously said to me, "I want to plead guilty."

Intending to calm her down, I said, "OK, just hold on." I informed the District Judge (DJ) that I needed a short recess as there seemed to be some change in the instructions from my client. The DJ agreed and I went out of the courtroom with Teo. I asked her what the matter was and she said she wanted to plead guilty. I asked why, especially when the evidence against her so far was quite flimsy. I felt that she should not plead guilty. She persisted, saying she wanted to plead guilty to get her son out of trouble and to keep him from going to jail. I told her that if she pleaded guilty, then *she* would go to jail. I also reminded her that should she go to jail, the only person who would be able to look after her son was her sister who was suffering from cancer. I asked her for her final decision. She answered without hesitation, "I'd rather go to jail than see my son go to jail."

Unfortunately, I had no choice when the instructions were such. I informed the DJ that we were changing our plea and she would be pleading guilty. I asked the DPP whether he was prepared to accept the original sentence for the charge of abetting an act of arson. He turned down our request. You know, many of these DPPs, when they know you are down they don't hesitate to kick you. Here, he knew the reason why she decided to plead guilty. He was not going to give way. I said, "You know why she is pleading guilty. Between you and me, you know that she is doing it not out of convenience but because of her love for her son. Why don't you take that into consideration and see whether you can go back to the original offer? They will still send her to jail but it will be for a shorter term." He refused to commit and said that he would confer with his senior DPP. Half an hour later, he came back and said that his instructions were to stick to the revised charge. He could not go back to the initial offer of a reduced charge as it had expired. He said, "Sorry, but you have to plead guilty for the current charge."

I explained to Teo that she could be in big trouble but she was insistent and willingly accepted the consequences. So she pleaded guilty and we submitted the psychiatrist's report. The DPP asked for a deterrent sentence, meaning a longer jail term. However, the DJ gave her six months, saying that the DPP's request was too high. We decided to go on appeal.

The High Court judge who heard the appeal reduced the sentence to two months. He was more compassionate than the DPP and the District Judge.

Again it shows that sometimes people do things without realising the consequences of their actions or they willingly accept blame because they do not want a loved one to get into trouble. They plead guilty for noble reasons. In this case, my client pleaded guilty to save her son. She didn't want him to go to jail. She'd rather go to jail herself than to see her son imprisoned.

A mother's love for her son can be very deep and this episode shows it so clearly. I could see the depth of her maternal love and I felt so sorry for her. There was only so much I could do for her. It was a decision she had to make. However, the prosecution couldn't see it and neither could the DJ. To them, a spade is a spade; white is white and black is black. There are no shades of grey. I cannot understand why the prosecution can be so hard-hearted and unwilling to understand the nature of the accused person or the motives behind the accused person's actions. If they could take that step, it would improve our legal system considerably.

We need to get DPPs who are experienced enough, who have seen the world and who understand the complexity of human nature, to come to the right decisions. Instead, we have a lot of what we, at the Defence Bar, call "scholar nerds" — these are people who don't understand anything except that it is the law and this is how it goes. They do not know how to exercise discretion.

FIVE

A SUDDEN LOSS

One afternoon, while I was at dialysis, I was given the sad news that Mr Karpal Singh, the lawyer whom I mentioned in my earlier book, had died in a car crash. I was very sad to hear that because he was a man whom I respected very much.

The last time I spoke with Karpal was when I had telephoned him, as President of the Association of Criminal Lawyers of Singapore, to invite him to come to Singapore to be one of the guest speakers for a Criminal Law Conference organised by the association.

He answered the phone, "Hey, how are you? I hope you are not in some trouble?" Amused, I replied, "No, I am not." I then explained the purpose of my call and he responded, "Of course, I will be there, but you have to give me proper notice as to when it is. Don't call me and tell me that the next day I have to be there like you did before. Give me sufficient notice and I will be there. Don't worry." He also added, "Come to think of it, in Malaysia, we don't have a criminal lawyers' association. I think we should start one." Agreeing with him, I said, "Yes, you should and maybe the two associations can work together on many issues." His last words to me then were, "That is a very interesting proposition, working together with you, Subhas. I think that is going to get a lot of people worried. But it's a good idea. I will think about it."

However, the conference had to be postponed and I telephoned him to tell him about it. We ended that conversation with him telling me to call him whenever I was next in Kuala Lumpur. Sadly, that was the last time I spoke with him.

When I heard that he had died in a traffic accident, I was very rattled and shaken by the tragic way he went and the fact that people can suddenly leave you. He was such a dynamic person. I will never forget this old friend of mine. His death led me to be more appreciative of all of my old friends.

There is a book written about him by Tim Donoghue. I have a copy, given to me by a mutual friend who said to me, "Read the book. You might like it, you might not like it." I read it. Donohue had mentioned an incident between Karpal Singh and me in Singapore University when we were both studying there. This incident was also mentioned in my earlier book.

Karpal loved fun. He enjoyed himself to the extent that he failed his exams a number of times. But it never bothered him. He gave people the impression that his whole purpose in life was to have a good time. Subsequently, when he graduated and went back to Malaysia, he changed. He entered politics and became a noted opposition member who showed people that he actually cared for them and that he had compassion for them. He took on difficult cases that nobody else wanted to do and he did the best he could. And that is why he left his footprint, not only in Malaysia's political world, but also in the legal arena. He went on to practise constitutional law and proved to the world that a person can be academically weak but when it came down to practice, it was a different game altogether. He was better than those who received first class honours or a second upper. He showed his true mettle in practice.

It is not going to be easy to find somebody to replace him. But then, Malaysia is a country that is capable of nurturing exceptional people. Let's hope that a replacement will be found as soon as possible. I have a lot of fond memories of Karpal.

I had wished to go to pay my last respects at his funeral but I couldn't make the trip to Malaysia because I had to undergo dialysis regularly. I myself nearly died because of my heart and kidney failure. Vimi offered to make the necessary arrangements if I really wanted to go as she could see that I was torn in my decision. But I said no as I felt that there was no point going when he was no more. I think Karpal would understand. He has always understood. But if I were well, I would attend his funeral because he was a man whom I cared for deeply. I wish his family all the best. I do not know how they are going to cope with such a loss but I suppose they have no choice but to do so. Stuck in my dialysis chair, I prayed for the soul of my dear friend who left us suddenly and very tragically. I thought of the past.

Some time in the early 1980s, I had asked Karpal to come and assist me in a contempt case involving the Workers' Party Chairman Wong Hong Toy. I gave him only 24 hours' notice. He cursed and swore at me but came that very evening. He went straight to JB Jeyaretnam's (JBJ) house so that he could prepare for the next morning's trial. That morning, we went to Court and argued the case the whole day until it was adjourned.

The sad part was JBJ did not even bother to host Karpal a lunch or dinner, much less meet him outside of Court for any social interaction. He gave a lot of excuses, saying that he had to meet his Party members and that he had other meetings and appointments. I felt really disappointed and upset, and I invited Karpal and his wife to dinner. I also invited them to lunch the next day before they left for the airport. I waited for them and when they arrived, Karpal looked at me and asked, "Subhas, why are you so glum today?" I just kept quiet.

He said, "You are upset because your client is not here?" I didn't answer him. He said, "You know, Subhas, don't ever be upset because of things like this. I did not come because I have any relationship with Jeyaretnam. I don't even know who he is. I have not moved with him socially. It doesn't matter whether he came and had lunch or dinner. I only came because of you as we have been friends since we read law in Bukit Timah campus. The spirit of the Union House that binds us will not allow me to let you down. Whenever you call me for help, I will come and I expect you to come when I call you. We all must have the spirit of helping each other. That is what made me. That's what it should be."

I just looked at him and thought to myself, "What a great guy he is, talking about Bukit Timah campus and the Union House." He expressed his feelings so eloquently to me. He essentially told me, "Look, you call, I will come and if I call, you must come." The bond will never be broken. So, you can imagine how I felt when I heard that he died in a car crash. I was so sad I wasn't able to say anything for some time because he is a man who doesn't deserve to die like that — in a horrific car crash. But that is how life is. We cannot predict the way we are going to go. Maybe we can influence the way we live, but how we go, we can never know. God bless Karpal Singh and may his spirit live on forever in Malaysian history.

It is so ironical that while I am thinking about Karpal during my dialysis, there sitting opposite me, is retired judge, Sam Sinnathuray, before whom Karpal and I appeared in that contempt case. On the opposing side of that trial were the Attorney-General Tan Boon Teik and DPP Glenn Knight. A week after Karpal left Singapore, Sam Sinnathuray delivered his judgement and he found Wong Hong Toy, Chairman of the Workers' Party, guilty of contempt and fined him S$8,000.

Today, I am sitting in this chair dictating while the judge is sitting ten metres away from me, watching television during his dialysis.

SIX

THE GOOD, THE BAD
AND THE UGLY

The Association of Criminal Lawyers of Singapore (ACLS) publishes a newsletter called *Pro Bono* which discusses the law and the changes to it. In one of the editorials, I reiterated what Sim Yong Chan, the editor of *Pro Bono*, once said — that we are living in a golden era for criminal law. For instance, members of the judiciary are changing. We have Chief Justice Sundaresh Menon, who was a practising lawyer before, and we have the then Attorney-General Steven Chong, who was also a practising lawyer with some experience in criminal law practice. To top that, we have K Shanmugam, Minister for Law and Foreign Affairs, who formerly practised criminal law. With these three people leading the judicial landscape, changes are expected and changes have come about. I have sat on two Committees: the Criminal Law Committee, which repealed the Criminal Procedure Code and drafted a new Code; and the Penal Code Committee, which considered mandatory death sentencing and decided that for certain offences, the judges will be given discretion whether to impose the death sentence.

Mandatory death sentencing is something I have been fighting against for a long time. I am not against the death sentence but I am against the mandatory death sentence. I have always felt that judges should be given the discretion to choose between a death sentence or life imprisonment. If you don't give them a choice and if you tie their hands, you are not allowing them to use their discretion. In my opinion, I believe that the golden era for changes to the criminal law started even before Sundaresh Menon became Chief Justice, while the rest slowly came into the picture.

VK Rajah, Justice of Appeal, who also heard Magistrate Court appeals, set the trend of discretionary judgement. He looked at judgements from the Subordinate Courts, many of which he reversed. He was a judge who earned the respect of the Criminal Bar with his decisive judgement and precise explanations of his conclusions and interpretation of the law. I have always appreciated him and the clarity he brought with his judgements. He, I would argue, was the first to start pushing the envelope, bringing about changes in the Criminal Procedure Code and the Penal Code. Nobody seems to realise that. Everybody talks about other people. Unfortunately, he is not hearing Magistrate Court appeals anymore.

On the other hand, we have certain judges who make me wonder how they were selected to sit as High Court Judges. For some of them, I would not even select them to sit in the Subordinate Courts as a Magistrate. They do not write proper judgements. Some of them write judgements that are only one page long, while others write on for 84 pages after sentencing a person to death. There should be a limit. There is a need to shorten their briefs, but not to one page, and to convey their judgements with clarity and precision. Some of these judges don't realise this. Nowadays, the judgements are so long, you wonder why you need to read them and how they are to be reproduced in the law magazines. Hundreds of pages long — I don't know what these judges are trying to achieve! They do get carried away. I remember when I was a student, we were afraid of reading Supreme Court judgements from India as their judgements could go on to be a tome; one could have a book out of the judgement. Things here are coming to this stage. I think if you can't say what you want to say in 20 to 30 pages, something is wrong. Anything more will just be a waste of time. It should be insisted that the brief be, well, brief. It often happens now that we ask an intern to read and summarise for us because the essence of the judgement is lost when the judge gets too long-winded.

In a particular case, a professor from the National University of Singapore was charged for corruption. His case was heard before the then Chief District Judge (CDJ). I felt that the CDJ's conduct of the case was not satisfactory and that he was being very high-handed. The defence counsel was not given sufficient time to subpoena the psychiatrist but still managed to produce him in court. In the end, the CDJ convicted the professor on all the charges and wrote a long judgement. Before the appeal came on, he was promoted to be a Judicial Commissioner of the High Court. When his judgement came up for appeal, it was heard before Justice Woo Bih Li. Justice Woo heard both sides of the argument and made a brilliant judgement, declaring the original judgement wrong because of confusion over certain vital points. He wondered why this could have happened.

So, you start to wonder how certain people get promoted when they can't even interpret the law of corruption properly. They rise as District Judges, sit there and get further promoted. What other greater mistakes can we make? And so, you have to take chances. In the Subordinate Court, I have taken some judges to the Court of Appeal on numerous occasions and got their judgements reversed. Yet, they still remain there, making the same old judgements which always get overruled in the end. As a defence counsel, it irks me to have to deal with such situations on a regular basis. More has to be looked into to ensure that the system can be fine-tuned to benefit all.

I found that dictating while doing dialysis is not as easy as I thought. You see, together with other patients, you watch nurses walking up and down monitoring us. Suddenly, you realise that you are totally dependant on the dialysis machine for your life. Then, depression hits and you wonder why you have to go through this stage and there are even times when you curse God. But, there are times when you pray to Him. It's all a confused state of mind. Sometimes, you even wonder about the existence of God and whether you are actually going to something that does or doesn't exist. But deep inside, with my religious upbringing and the fact that I am the Chairman of the Board of Trustees of a Hindu temple, there lies a conviction within me that there is a God and God works in mysterious ways. You really do not understand some of the things He does but again you must learn to accept it. The process of accepting is difficult but slowly I am getting the knack of it.

SEVEN

PUSHED TO THE BRINK

The case of Ong Pang Siew is a very unusual one. Ong Pang Siew met here in Singapore a woman named Xiu from the People's Republic of China in 1997 and they married in 2002. They have a son.

Xiu wanted to bring her daughter from her previous marriage to Singapore to study. Ong was very obliging. The daughter came and the whole family stayed together. Ong gave her all the fatherly support that he could think of. He looked after her financially and treated her like a daughter, always caring and supportive of her.

Unfortunately, the marriage broke down when Ong found out that his wife was fooling around, going out late in the night to KTV lounges, and coming back with different men. Ong granted Xiu a divorce in May 2007 and left the family home. Xiu was given custody of their son. Ong was always very agitated at the fact that his ex-wife was not looking after their son properly. He found that she had no time to care for their son. She was spending too much time outside the home. While his 15-year-old stepdaughter from China could look after herself, the same couldn't be said for the boy who was very young then. It also didn't help that his ex-wife always made it difficult for Ong to see his son on weekends. Ong had to go to her workplace or to different venues on her suggestions to pick up his son. The situation made him very frustrated and angry.

One weekend, when he wanted to see his son, he found out that his ex-wife had taken him to her workplace. Ong told her to bring the boy to the flat so that he could pick him up from there. She said, "If you are interested in seeing him, you come here." She was very curt and slammed down the phone. Ong was angry. He cycled to her flat, the very place where he used to stay and found his stepdaughter there. She opened the door for him and they talked. What began as a normal conversation got so heated that he pushed her to the floor, banged her head against the floor and repeatedly shouted at her, "Who am I?" This was witnessed by a sub-tenant who came out of her room on hearing the girl's screams.

Ong then realised what he had done. He called his brother to say that he had killed his stepdaughter and that he wanted to commit suicide. He also called his employer and apologised for not being able to go to work. The sub-tenant called Xiu, who called the police.

When the police arrived, they found him squatting by her body, crying and talking incoherently. His conduct showed that there was something mentally wrong with him. We were briefed to represent him. We requested a psychiatrist to examine Ong so as to ascertain whether there was anything wrong with him mentally. If so, we needed to know what mental illness Ong had.

During the trial, the psychiatrist Dr Tommy Tan testified that he had diagnosed Ong as suffering from major depressive disorder. His report identified that Ong had many of the symptoms of major depressive disorder and qualified for the diagnosis. Of course, the psychiatrist appointed by the prosecution, Dr Jerome Goh from the Institue of Mental Health (IMH) came up with an entirely different diagnosis, saying that there was nothing wrong with Ong and that he was perfectly normal.

Given those two different reports and that many of the other facts of the case were disputed, the charge of the crime should differ too. Justice Tay Yong Kwang decided to accept IMH's psychiatric report; he convicted Ong and sentenced him to death. We had no choice but to take the matter up to the Court of Appeal.

At the Court of Appeal, we put forward the same argument, explaining why Ong should not have been sentenced to death and arguing that the charge of murder was wrong. It should have been culpable homicide because he was suffering from Diminished Responsibility. The prosecution argued against us. They referred to the IMH psychiatric report and said that there was nothing wrong with Ong. Fortunately, the Court of Appeal agreed with our argument that Ong was suffering from a mental illness. In fact, it was the Court of Appeal that told the prosecution to look at Ong's symptoms and the circumstances of the case.

Looking at these various factors, the Court said, it should be realised that this person was actually suffering from Diminished Responsibility. The Court of Appeal also commented that Dr Tommy Tan was a much more experienced psychiatrist when compared to Dr Jerome Goh, who was younger and less experienced. Thus, Dr Tan's report should not have been ignored. The appeal was allowed and Ong was ordered to go back to the judge that had initially sentenced him.

At the sentencing hearing, the prosecution asked for life imprisonment on the basis that Ong was a very dangerous person who could not be trusted to behave himself if he was released early. Thankfully, the judge was not prepared to accept that. He accepted our argument that Ong had been behaving himself while in prison; he had been taking his medicines regularly; he had been cooperating with the authorities; and he was in remission and getting better. The judge then sentenced Ong to ten years' imprisonment effective from the day he was arrested.

His family was curious about what would happen to him. When I saw his ex-wife and son, she gave me a look that, if looks could kill, I would have been dead! I walked away, knowing that in our profession, you can't please everyone!

Ong Pang Siew was suffering from a disease — major depressive disorder — without realising it. As this disease does not manifest itself physically, those afflicted may not be diagnosed and get treatment early. Certain symptoms may appear but if you are not an expert or if you have not had any interaction with others afflicted with the disease, you will find it very hard to determine if a person has depression.

Even those who were with Ong regularly, including his drinking buddies, didn't realise that he was suffering from this disease. To them, Ong was a very happy-go-lucky person, who always seemed to be in a good mood, drinking a lot of beer. Although they did notice that he was losing some weight, and losing weight is one of the systems of major depressive disorder, nobody realised it at that time. He was dealing with multiple emotions — feeling sad, betrayed and depressed. So without any premeditation, he went and committed this crime. He released all his frustration on his stepdaughter who provoked him in a heated argument.

What do you do in this situation? Our system recognises that Diminished Responsibility is a defence. One must be very careful to come to a conclusion that a person is suffering from Diminished Responsibility because the wrong analysis can lead to the wrong punishment. I ask myself, "Do I think Ong Pang Siew should go to jail for ten years, especially when he is suffering from Diminished

Responsibility? Is our system sufficient to look after people like Ong?" These are some of the questions I keep on asking and I find no answers.

Sometimes, I do think that even if an accused person is suffering from a mental disease, he or she should be locked up for good because of the violent nature of the offence. Sometimes, I feel that we have to be more understanding. We still have the McNaughton rule — when mental capacity is successfully raised as a defence either because the defendant did not know what he was doing or that it was wrong — which has been around for years.

Once, in a jovial way, I asked the Law Minister, "Mr Shanmugam, why are we keeping the McNaughton rule even now?" He reflected that the last time he heard about the McNaughton rule, he was a student attending a lecture. I responded, "Exactly, so why do we keep it when the definition has become totally irrelevant?" He replied, "We have to look into it." When he says he will look into it, he will really look into it.

EIGHT

AT DEATH'S DOOR

I have just instructed Diana and Sunil to bring me the relevant files for the cases I want to discuss in my book. Without the files, it's very difficult for me to write the details about the cases. Those files are either in the office or in the warehouse. While I wait for the files, let me tell you about a significant event that happened to me in December 2008, soon after I launched my first book.

Vimi went on a cruise with her siblings. She had asked me whether she should go with them and whether I could manage without her for those few days. I assured her, "Yes, I will be fine. You should go have a break from me because you look a bit tired. The cruise will cheer you up." So she left.

I was a little relieved as she was holding such a tight control over me, sometimes it's so tight that I feel I cannot breathe. I thought to myself, "Ah, this is an opportunity to have some fun."

I spent late nights with my friends enjoying ourselves in harmless fun. We went to karaoke nightclubs and had late night suppers. I could come back at whatever time I felt like coming back because there was nobody waiting for me at home. The day before Vimi returned, my nephew, Sunil, suggested having a drink with another colleague. So we went to one of those bars near UOB Plaza and decided to have margaritas.

The first margarita that came for me made me very unhappy because they used the wrong glass, there was not enough salt in the drink, and the margarita did not taste like margarita. So I told my colleague that the whole thing was wrong and started explaining to her how margaritas should be made. She spoke to the bartender about my displeasure. Soon after, a waitress came with a proper salt-rimmed glass. I took a sip and declared, "*This* is a margarita." They didn't charge me for the first one. I had two drinks and then decided to have one more, the last drink, they call it, "one for the road". Sunil took me home. I didn't have dinner because of the finger food we had with our margaritas.

Early the next morning, I started to cough. I thought it was one of those things that come and go. So I went to work as usual. By the time I got home from work, the coughing had become more incessant and my son, who was at home said, "Pa, what's happening? Are you OK?" I replied, "Ya, sure, I am OK". Aware that he was going out with his friends, I assured him, "No need for you to cancel your plans. Don't worry about me, son."

He was in his room getting dressed when Vimi returned. She put her luggage down by the door, looked at me and said, "What's wrong? How are you?" I turned around, still coughing incessantly. I could see she was getting anxious. She knew that it was more than just a cough as I was wheezing as well. I am not asthmatic. She asked, "When did this cough start?" I told her it started sometime in the morning but it seemed to be getting worse. She asked, "What have you been doing?" Sheepishly, I suggested that I may be having a 'gas problem' and told her, "Uh, the maid gave me some ginger water and I also drank some Omum (Indian tonic)." Observing me further, she said, "This is not good. I don't like the sound of your persistent wheezy cough. I think your heart is failing. You're going to the hospital now!" With my usual shrug-off attitude, I told her, "No, don't make a big fuss." This time she refused to give in. She called Chechy, who was then an anaesthetist in Alexandra Hospital, and described my situation to her. Chechy said to take me straight to Alexandra Hospital. She said she was off duty but she would be there. She called her colleague to expect our arrival at the hospital and do what was necessary. Vimi and Sujesh rushed me there.

By the time I got to the hospital's A&E department, I was gasping for air and it was getting more and more difficult to breathe. I felt as though I was drowning; I didn't know it then but my lungs were waterlogged. My heart was failing and my situation critical. It was decided that I had to be immediately admitted to the Intensive Care Unit (ICU) where I was infused with diuretic drugs to flush the fluid from my lungs to ease my breathing. I was also supported with oxygen. Quite swiftly, the medical team in the ICU were circling around me and suddenly I saw all sorts of tubes being inserted into me.

Prior to this medical attention, the wait to be pushed to ICU seemed long and endless. I called my son over and said to him, "Don't let this worry you. It is not a big matter. But, my son, promise me one thing as I may not survive this. Promise me that you must always listen to your mother and be together with her." He assured me, "Yes, Pa, I will always be with Mummy." I told him, "There is no need for you to remain in the hospital as you are of no help here. Why don't you join your friends and keep your phone on so that you can be contacted any time." He said, "I don't want to go." I insisted, "No, I think you better go because it would take your mind off things. I should be alright." Then he left my bedside to be with his mother.

I beckoned Vimi to come over. "Come, I want to tell you something." She came close, leaned forward and I said, "I see your face in every rose, I see your smile in every cloud," and then I dozed off for a while. I must have left my poor wife in a state of confusion. She wondered what that all meant as I have never been one for romantic words.

When I awoke, I also noticed that my siblings and my sister-in-law, Syon, were waiting outside, too. They all looked very worried. As I was being wheeled to ICU, I held their hands, reassuring them that I would be alright.

Chechy has always been emotionally very strong but my younger sister, Sugadha, is not. I could see tears in her eyes. I remember telling her, "Don't worry, everything will be alright." Then I saw my brother, Sudheesh, in the distance, looking calm and steady. He just nodded to me and I nodded back at him. We never have much to say to each other but our actions speak volumes. His nod to me was a signal not to worry and that everything will be all right. It also assured me that they were all there for me. For all the tragedies or near tragedies in our lives, I realise how lucky I am for having such a close-knit family with such a strong bond.

I was thinking then, that if my late brother, Surash, was around, he would also be there. He would be standing close by without saying a word but exuding assurance that he was there for all of us. Unfortunately, this time, he was no longer around like he had always been for me whenever I was hospitalised. It had become a habit for me to turn around to see where he was. I still unconsciously look for him, only to realise that he is not around any more. That feeling of realisation, that he is not around, always makes me want to cry. We are all so close, he being the youngest in the family, made it even harder.

I spent that night in the ICU which seemed like one of the longest nights in my life as I was not able to leave the bed at all — complete rest in bed. Miraculously, the next morning I felt a lot better. My lungs were clear again and I could breathe easily. By 8:00 am, I was getting restless from being constrained to the bed in ICU. As usual, I always like to negotiate with my doctors. I explained that if they wanted me to recover quickly, it would be best to send me to the ward. This is not an easy request for any doctor to accommodate but they relented when I agreed to wear a monitoring device on me so that they could keep full surveillance on my cardiac condition. My lungs were also cleared of fluid. By 9:00 am, with this gadget on, they allowed me to be in the ward. I called Vimi to inform her that I was in the ward and not in ICU which obviously surprised her. Seemingly pleased but her first reaction was, "Did you negotiate to leave or the doctor ordered it voluntarily?" That is how well she knew me. I laughed and said that I had negotiated but was prepared to wear the 24-hour cardiac monitor.

The cardiologist said that I was lucky to have come to the hospital on time, that I would have died if I remained at home. Once again, Vimi was perceptive and did the right thing. I was on medical leave for some time.

I asked Vimi, "Do you remember what I told you?" She said "Ya, it was so unlike you. You told me that my face is in every rose, my smile in every cloud. What was I to make of this? I thought you had a secret code to share with me at death's door!" She mentioned that it was the first time she felt that I might not make it. After I was pushed to the ICU, she went outside, sat down and cried, something she doesn't do easily even at the worse of times. And I said, "You have always accused me of not being romantic, but you see, at least when I thought that I was going to die, I did my best to please you!"

NINE

YOUR SMILE IN EVERY CLOUD

March 2014. One of the side effects of dialysis is the occasional lack of appetite. Sometimes I tell Vimi, "I want to eat Japanese. I feel very hungry." She would be so thrilled by the fact that I was asking for food that she would take me anywhere just to feed me. However, once the food is placed before me, I would not be hungry anymore. I would feel nauseous and Vimi would get upset that I was not eating. She would try to coax me into eating, insisting that I needed to eat to build my strength. She was afraid that if I lacked energy, I would not even attempt simple exercises like walking. So, I would force myself to eat. There is no pleasure and I would feel even more depressed. Vimi would try all ways to talk me out of it with her positive words and smiles. But it was hard although I wanted so much to do it for her.

Another side effect is insomnia. I would sit in the living room, yawn, and feel very tired and sleepy. I would go into the bedroom. Vimi faithfully always accompanies me to make sure that I was tucked in properly and I would try to sleep. But I cannot sleep. I would lie awake from 10:00 pm till 6:00 am the next morning, just wondering what was going to happen to my life; and thinking of what has already happened. I think of the past; I think of the present; I think of the future; but it's all muddled up. It's also confusing and I know that I could sink low into depression again.

I would be thinking of the future, then I would be thinking of the past, the happy times that I had and I would think, "You are luckier than most people in the sense that you have a good life, a good wife and son, good siblings, and good friends who stood by you. What else can you ask for? You can't have everything." Vimi reminds me, "When you were supposed to leave us in December and a doctor even recommended palliative care, we didn't want to listen to him. We insisted that you get the best care till you were out of the woods. God doesn't want you to die, not in December 2013. He has saved you for a particular reason. In time to come, you will see the reason, but in the meantime, you should not be depressed."

Vimi has been a pillar of sense and strength for me. Every day I would bug her. I tried to pass all my misery to her. She would take it very gracefully and tell me how important I am in her life and my family's life and that I should not give up. I should not just talk about dying. There was a purpose in living. She is a source of encouragement and my son, while in Nottingham, sends short messages to me through his mother, as I don't possess a cell phone, to remind me that there is somebody there who wants me alive. Suddenly I somehow want to see him graduate. I won't be lucky enough to see him get married and have children but I said to God, "God, at least let me see my son graduate. That is the least you can do for me. After all, I am not such a bad person. I have done good things in my life". I kept on saying that to God. But, sometimes I feel that He doesn't hear anymore. I feel that I have been abandoned by God. But I suppose we will never know what plan God has for us.

I take consolation in knowing that Vimi is always lying beside me, massaging my back to ease the pain that I constantly have from sitting at dialysis. She does this for me every night in the hope that I would

Vimi and Subhas enjoying a quiet moment on their garden swing.

fall asleep, and sometimes I do for a short while. I find listening to music every night at bedtime very soothing and comforting. Vimi had compiled a selection of my favourite songs that includes Hindi, Tamil, Malayalam and English songs. My choices lately are more meaningful and less upbeat. The one song that I must listen to every night, at least three to four times, is "If Tomorrow Never Comes" by Ronan Keating. On listening to the lyrics again and again, one night Vimi asked if it spoke my sentiment. I told her, "Yes, every single word." I am not good at expressing how I feel for her but the words to this song speaks volumes. I hope when she listens to it, she takes comfort in knowing how I feel for her.

TEN

YOU ARE MY SUNSHINE

Some time ago, Phang Wah also known as James Phang, was almost nominated 'Businessman of the Year'. His enterprise, one he personally built up, was called Sunshine Empire Private Limited. However, before he was given the nomination, he was called up by the Commercial Affairs Department (CAD) on suspicion of knowingly carrying on the business of Sunshine Empire for the fraudulent purpose of selling prime packages supposedly yielding high returns to trusting eager investors, or subscribers for thousands and maybe even millions of dollars. Many other people were arrested, and subsequently his wife, Madam Neo Kuon Huay, and his friend, Jackie Hoo Choon Cheat, were charged under various sections of the Companies Act (Cap 50) as well as the Penal Code.

The scheme was not a new one. It was an old scheme known as 'pyramid selling' with a new twist. Previously, pyramid selling was considered illegal because subscribers got nothing in return for the money they paid to the company. In this particular case, Sunshine Empire gave subscribers a packet of goodies and discounts for joining. The company claimed that the profits were shared between them and the subscribers. Upon payment of subscription, the returns could be as high as from 30 per cent to 40 per cent. The success of the Scheme could be attributed to Madam Neo, who was referred to as the First

Lady of Sunshine. She was alleged to have brought in millions of dollars.

Word got around that Sunshine Empire paid very good interest rates or profits if money was invested with them. Soon, there was a stampede of people rushing to the company's office with cash and cheques. People were withdrawing large sums of money from their bank accounts, and the banks began to wonder what was happening. In time, they found out that Sunshine Empire was collecting these monies. The banks realised that they were losing a lot of customers due to this promise of high returns that could not be matched by any legal financial institution. It was just financially impossible for them to match Sunshine Empire's promises.

It was subsequently proven in Court that a day would come when Phang and Sunshine Empire would not be able to meet their obligations as they would run out of money; this was because the company did not operate any substantive profit generating business, and therefore had no sustainable means of funding the high returns paid out to subscribers.

An expert in forensic accounting from London who came to Singapore and gave evidence for the prosecution was not impressive. He said that this type of business woud definitely not be sustainable and was doomed to fail. When I cross-examined him, he said that there was a possibility that any business could fail and that a company that officially looked very good could end up failing, while a company that looked bad on paper could become successful when the management turned it around with new ideas and new people. As far as the defence was concerned, his evidence was neither here nor there.

The expert that we engaged from Hong Kong gave evidence that Sunshine Empire could succeed provided certain remedial actions were undertaken. Further, he felt that it was too premature for CAD to arrest those involved because arresting them would destroy the company. In fact, when I cross-examined the CAD's officer-in-charge, I said that in the event these people were acquitted on the basis that they had not done anything wrong, his department would be sued the millions of dollars which the Sunshine Empire and the subscribers lost. He had no response and just kept quiet.

Finally, after numerous arguments and testimonials, a fair number of investors felt that they were misled while others said they invested because they believed in the company. Looking at all the evidence presented, District Judge Jasvender Kaur found all three guilty. Subsequently, she sentenced Phang to nine years' imprisonment and Hoo to six months. As for Madam Neo, she was given a fine, even though the prosecution asked for a custodial sentence. We applied for bail, pending appeal. It was granted.

The appeal was heard before Justice Tay Yong Kwang. Even though Justice Tay has a reputation for being a tough judge, meting out sentences that can be higher than what other judges would give, he was quite fair in this case. He's a very experienced judge, having presided over many criminal cases. He reserved his judgement, taking into account the prosecution's appeal that Phang's sentence was too low and that Neo should have been sent to jail. Eventually, Justice Tay dismissed both the appeals brought by the defence and the prosecution.

I decided to pose some questions of public interest. Strangely enough, Justice Tay agreed with me that there were questions of public interest that had to be heard by the Court of Appeal. He dismissed one out of the five questions that I posed and referred the four questions to the Court of Appeal. Later, Mr Philip Fong, counsel for the co-accused, Jackie Hoo, wrote in for permission to refer the same questions to the

Court of Appeal. Justice Tay said that since permission was granted
to James Phang, Jackie Hoo should be allowed as well.

As I started to present my case at the Court of Appeal, which
comprised Justices of Appeal VK Rajah, Andrew Phang and Chao Hick
Tin, Justice of Appeal VK Rajah asked me in his usual very candid way,
"Mr Anandan, I do not know about my colleagues, but I believe that
there is no question of public interest, so what is your position?" I said,
"If you believe and if your colleagues believe that there is no question
of public interest, then there is nothing more to argue." He looked at
me, smiled and before I could continue with my comment, they asked
Philip Fong for his opinion. Philip Fong argued that since Justice Tay
had referred the case to the Court of Appeal, the Court of Appeal had
no choice but to answer the questions of public interest.

The Justices had to determine whether they had the power to dismiss
our application. It was a very important point that I emphasised when
I was asked to continue with my submissions. I started arguing on the
law and the facts, and Justice of Appeal Andrew Phang, if I remember
correctly, asked me, "Do you agree that if we decided that there was
no question of public interest, we don't have to listen to this appeal?" I
very candidly told him, "You are right. If this Court decides there is no
question of public interest, whatever Justice Tay said is not relevant."

They replied that they would make up their minds immediately
after listening to the DPP. I pleaded with them, "Please consider
these points once more before you make up your mind." Fortunately,
they agreed. They adjourned for half an hour. But when they came
back, they said, "We have decided that we should not accept your
arguments because we don't agree that there are questions of public
interest, but out of deference to counsel, we will answer the questions."
Unfortunately, all the answers were not good for the clients.

The purpose of including this case in this book is to show what human greed can lead to. It is sad that there will always be people who try and capitalise on the greed of others. The people who bought into Sunshine Empire and lost money are not just ordinary people. Some of them are senior financial controllers and financial analysts. They are professionals who went into this scheme thinking they would make some quick money. When I cross-examined them, I would always ask whether they had read the clause in their contract with Sunshine Empire which said that the return of investment was at the discretion of the company. Did they understand what they were signing? They said they knew but did not pay any attention to it because they were attracted by the returns they would get. They didn't think it was an important issue when they signed the contract. Hundreds of people lost money. Some of them lost all their savings; some lost even their CPF savings that were withdrawn to invest with Sunshine Empire. Some of them borrowed money from their friends and relatives so that they could invest. All because they thought they were going to make quick money.

This incident shows that Singaporeans, and people generally, still have a lot to learn. They need to know that it is not easy to make money, as made out in the way the scheme was advertised. There is nothing like hard work.

James Phang Wah is a brilliant man and I think he is one person who could have done very well in any venture that he chose to start. I am very sure that if he were to use the intelligence he has wisely, he could have started a venture that would have made him very rich, the legal way. Unfortunately, he decided to take a shortcut, thinking that he could outsmart everybody, including the authorities. In fact, during his confrontation with the Consumers Association of Singapore

(CASE), when people were advised against investing money with Sunshine Empire, he still managed to convince potential investors that CASE was mistaken about his company. CASE was a bit taken aback by Phang and his associates' aggressive stand.

Phang and his associates decided to contact CAD themselves to set up a meeting with them to clear certain issues. They wanted to explain their actions and defend the legality of their investment ventures. The CAD were prepared to have a meeting with them. However, when Phang, Hoo and the rest went for the meeting, they were promptly arrested.

When I cross-examined the CAD's officer-in-charge, he admitted that they had misled them so that they would go to the CAD. I said, "You didn't have to lie. They wanted to go to CAD anyway as they wanted to have a meeting with you. So why do you have to resort to such actions?" I told him that if Phang and his associates were acquitted, the chances are he would be sued, and his department would be sued for destroying the ongoing Sunshine Empire that was supporting hundreds of people.

ELEVEN

SECOND CHANCE

I seldom take on cases from other lawyers unless I have no choice. It makes it even worse when I have to take over cases from good friends.

On one occasion, a father walked in to my office and said, "My son is being charged for culpable homicide and he needs a lawyer." I said, "If it is culpable homicide, have you been given a lawyer by the court as his original charge was murder?" He replied, "Yes, but before the lawyer could do anything, it was the prosecutor who reduced the charges to culpable homicide. The person who is acting for my son now is Peter Fernando. My son wants you to take over the case from him."

I asked the father, "Why do you want to change lawyers? He's been doing all the work. I am sure he will be able to do a good job. I know him personally and I know his father personally too." He replied, "I do not want to change lawyers myself as I, too, am a friend of Peter Fernando. I have gone to his house, we have shared a few drinks together and have become good friends. But my son, who is in prison, insists that I must change lawyers and you must be the one." If you don't accept the brief, he will still insist that I find someone else to replace Peter Fernando. So what do you say?"

I replied, "Alright, we will come to a compromise. Don't discharge Peter Fernando. I will do the argument of sentencing and Peter

Fernando will do whatever arguments there are to be done. He will talk about the background and how this offence of culpable homicide came about." The father said he would talk to his son.

When he came back to me, he said that his son was agreeable to this arrangement but he still wanted me to take the role of the lead counsel. Reassuringly, I replied, "Yes. I will be the lead counsel because I will be arguing the sentence. There is nothing to argue in this case because the prosecutor has already reduced the charge to culpable homicide."

The father accepted the arrangement and I met with his son, Sadayan Ajmeershah. A pleasant young man. He and I got along well. I asked him, "Why do you want me to do the sentence?" He said, "Well, I heard about your reputation while here in prison and I think I got a better chance if you do my mitigation on sentence."

"Fair enough," I replied.

We went to court and the same statement of facts was read by the prosecution. After Peter had finished his explanation of what happened, I took over and argued why the sentence should not be life imprisonment. I argued for the courts to be fair. "You should give him ten years. There is no need to punish him so hard with life imprisonment," I argued.

You must remember that at that time, judges could only choose between imposing a sentence of up to ten years or life imprisonment. There was nothing in-between. That came about only after long campaigning, and countless dialogues with the prosecution and with the Minister for Law. The minister finally accepted the arguments and allowed judges to impose a sentence of up to 20 years' imprisonment or life imprisonment. But prior to this change of law and at the time of this trial, it was either up to ten years or life imprisonment.

The most startling thing about the mitigation was my client's letter to the court. He said to the judge, "I did not know how much my father loves me. I only realised how much he loves me when I saw how he was going around looking for lawyers, begging them to help me. I suddenly realised that the man who has shown no affection to me all these years, actually loves me deeply." He said that the realisation of how much his father loved him was very important. Now that he knew how much his father cared for him, he wanted a second chance, to show that he was remorseful and to try and help his father financially, morally and in every other way possible.

I think the judge was very touched by the letter and told the accused, "Well, it takes a tragedy like this for you to realise how much your father loves you. Even though your lawyer asked that I should give only ten years, and not to give life imprisonment, I will give you nine years. I will take away one year. Originally, I wanted to give you ten years. But I am looking at the mitigation, reading the letter and I feel that there should be a further reduction. So I am giving you nine years."

Everybody was happy. I told Sadayan that he was lucky the judge was very sympathetic because of his letter. He said, "Mr Anandan, everything I said in the letter is true. To me, my father's love is the most important thing. All my life, I grew up thinking that my father never loved me. After I got into this trouble, I now realise how much he cared for me. Surprisingly, I realise how much he means to me too."

With deep concern for his future, I asked Sadayan, "What do you intend to do?" He said, "When I come out of prison, I will be a reformed person. I will not hang out with those people whom I have been befriending and getting into trouble with. I will try and get a good job. I will do my best to help my father financially. I will return to him the money that he has spent on me." He added, "Thank you very much, Mr Anandan. I understand you charged my father only a nominal fee and I thank you for the low fees. People in prison told me that your fees are high but I know now that it is not true. I know that you are a man with a kind heart. I hope one day, I will be able to repay you."

Then he said to me earnestly, "You only have one kidney, do you want a kidney from me?" I was a little irritated but grateful. I said, "No. I did not help you for that." I added, "I helped you because I know that you are not a bad person. You were thrown into circumstances which made you do things which you otherwise would not do." As I needed to hear his commitment to reform, I asserted, "Keep your promise. Look after your father as he is getting old. I sincerely hope that when you come out, you will look after him."

He promised, "Yes, Mr Anandan, I will look after my father. I will visit you too." Feeling a sense of relief that he would do good on a second chance, I thanked him.

It is hearing such repentance and promises to reform that makes my work so meaningful. I always feel that society at large is very judgemental about ex-inmates. Some of them are genuinely eager to turn over a new leaf. It is very sad when, in all reality, it becomes hard when they try to get back on track but fail to do so as they have already been ostracised by society. Inevitably, without proper guidance and support, many fall back into a life of crime to survive. I hope that some time soon, society will become more understanding and compassionate, and welcome them back into the fold.

TWELVE

REBELS OF THE 1970S

Tan Wah Piow was a student leader in the 1970s. He, along with a girl called Juliet Chin, led the students' movement against the authorities on things that they perceived to be unfair or unconstitutional. When I left university in 1970, together with friends like Sim Yong Chan and Sunny Chew, we were under the impression that there would be no one else to carry on creating this kind of so-called 'trouble' against the authorities. We were all young and idealistic and shared a common dislike for the authorities. But, we were resigned that what has to be, has to be, and if the students' movement was going to die, so be it. So, I was pleasantly surprised when I found that there were still people, like Wah Piow and Juliet, 'rebelling' in the university.

Francis Khoo was one of my good friends. He had run away to London when he was pursued by the Internal Security Department. Once he approached me and suggested, "We should give the current students' movement whatever help they want." I replied, "When you say whatever help, it all depends, you know. I cannot just give a blank cheque and say, go and cash it. You ought to be careful. They may be genuine people but you do not know how far it can go." However, when Wah Piow and Juliet got into trouble with the immigration authorities, I went with Juliet to get her passport released. The immigration authorities were not happy about it but I told them that if they did not release her passport, we would take this matter to court the next day. An immigration officer called me and reluctantly released her passport. Before handing it to me, he said, "You know that Juliet Chin is not a Singaporean. She is a foreigner and she is here to incite trouble. I replied, "Never mind about that." I took her passport and left.

Subsequently, in November 1974, Tan Wah Piow was charged for inciting a riot against one of the unions in Singapore. Originally, it was decided that I would appear as counsel for him, but then Francis Khoo and the rest thought that maybe Wah Piow should defend himself so that he could do and say whatever he liked as he would not be hindered by legal ethics. He could hide behind the shadows, since he did not have any legal training or legal obligations. Finally, it was decided that Wah Piow would defend himself. But, whenever possible, I would attend court with him, to assist him when necessary.

I faithfully went to court just in case Wah Piow needed my assistance. Most of the time though, it was to watch the proceedings. He was being prosecuted by Abdul Wahab Ghows, who was then the Solicitor General. It was very funny because the courtroom was divided into two sections — one section was where all the student supporters sat, while on the other side were all the trade union supporters.

During breaks, the trade union supporters brought coffee, tea, curry-puffs and samosas for themselves and for their counsel Mr Ghows. Mr Ghows would always invite me to join them, "Hey, you come here." I would go over and they would offer me a cup of tea and some curry-puffs. We would stand around and talk. This went on for a few days, and I was enjoying the hot snacks a lot.

However, one day, Ghows called me and said, "I can't give you coffee and tea anymore, neither can I give you any of the curry-puffs because I have been told by the trade union leaders that you are on the other side. Is that true?" I replied sheepishly, "Yes, it's true." He said, "All the more you shouldn't take any of our stuff." "Thank you and goodbye," I promptly said after finishing my snacks and tea and went back to sit in my chair near the student union leaders.

The case continued for many more days. I remember Francis Khoo was there defending one of the accused persons and G. Raman was defending another accused person. Subsequently, T.S. Sinnathuray, who was then the Senior District Judge (SDJ), convicted all the accused persons. To many within the legal circles, it was something that was expected. This was because Wah Piow had been giving the judge a lot of trouble during the proceedings. He would continuously interrupt cross-examinations or tell the judge that he was not being fair, accusing the judge of being biased. I actually admired the patience of SDJ Sinnathuray who took all that nonsense and continued presiding over the case.

At the end of the case in February 1975, when Wah Piow was convicted and sentenced to one year's imprisonment, he was asked if he had anything to say. He started out by saying that he would like to congratulate the judge for his future promotion to the High Court. That was the first time we saw SDJ Sinnathuray lose his temper. He said, "Don't be impertinent. Take him away from my court. He doesn't know how to behave. Let him be in the lock-up while I sentence him." So, he was taken away to the lock-up. Subsequently, SDJ Sinnathuray sentenced all of them after the mitigation plea, and Wah Piow received one year of imprisonment. He was taken to prison to serve his sentence.

In prison, he was treated well by the inmates and the wardens who were sympathetic towards him. At the end of his sentence, and after his release, without further ado, he was handed an enlistment order to serve National Service immediately. He requested, "Why don't you give me a break before I go and do my National Service?" They said, "No. Your time has come and you have to serve." I do not know whether he did his National Service or not because in 1976, he ran away from Singapore and went to London in exile. He was admitted to Oxford University and obtained his law degree there. I was told he did very well.

Subsequently, many years later in 1987, 16 people were arrested for Marxist conspiracy activities, which they denied. Wah Piow was the man that was identified as the brains behind the whole movement. It was all over the newspapers. I believe he was naturally very upset about it.

One day when I walked into my office after a matter in court, my secretary, all excited, said, "Tan Wah Piow telephoned and would like you to call him back. He is waiting for your phone call." Out of curiosity, I decided to return his call. "Yes, Wah Piow, what can I do for you?" He said, "I want you to sue the Government for making all sorts of defamatory remarks against me which are not true." I said, "Yes, I can do that but are you prepared to come back to Singapore to be present when the case is going on because you cannot fight in absence. Are you prepared?" He said, "What will happen to me when I come back to Singapore?" I said, "They will probably arrest you at the airport. So you think about it and let me know."

He said "OK", but he never called back again.

Only when you are in trouble, will you realise who your friends are. I learnt a very important lesson in 1976 when I was taken to jail. Friends whom I thought would stand by me, ran away. Those I did not know very well, came to my help; they were a source of moral support to my family and they surprised me with their courage in standing up against the authorities to say that I was innocent.

So when I fell ill last year, nothing should have surprised me. There were people whom I thought would come and visit me, sit with me and give me encouragement, but never did. Those whom I have lost touch with — my old classmates and dear friends who grew up with me — even though I have not seen them for years, once they knew that I was ill, they all made it a point to come to see me. They comforted me with encouraging words, told me that they would always be with me, not to worry and that they were all praying for me to get well.

On the other hand, there were those whom I considered like family, whom I thought were very close to me — they never came. I know I should not have any expectations of anyone but it was inevitable to feel disappointed when I was at the lowest point of my life. I would have done anything for them if they were in trouble because to me, friendship is something very deep and meaningful. I do not believe in fly-by-night friendships. Well, I don't blame these people. I don't blame people who never visited me or who didn't want to know anything about my condition. Different people react differently when their friends are sick. I know that if my friend is sick, I will surely visit him once or twice at least. I will pray for him. But whether I will visit him every day, I am not too sure because I am not the type who can go and sit with a sick friend and encourage him with nice, comforting words; but I will make sure my sick friend knows how I feel and wish him well.

Notwithstanding those who disappointed me, there were many who made me so happy, especially when I was in hospital. My wife would wheel me down to the canteen, sometimes with my siblings, to have a drink or a snack. Strangers who knew of me would approach me, hold my hand and wish me well. Some even assured me of their prayers.

Once while at dialysis, I was interrupted by a lady who was about to do her dialysis. She came to say she recognised me and that she was very sad to see me here. She said she would pray for my recovery and hope that I will continue helping people. Imagine that! The kindness of yet another stranger who needed prayers for herself for a speedy recovery too!

So the hundreds of people who came to greet me, wish me well and who said they would pray for me, made me very happy. So who cares about the people who disappointed me? It doesn't really matter. I know that out there, there are many who care for me, many who pray for me, many who want me to live. I think it's the combined prayers of all these people, including those of my family that made me defeat death in December 2013.

I truly appreciate the thoughtfulness and kindness of these people, some of whom are strangers. When I think of their words of encouragement and their support in prayers, my eyes would well up with tears. I find it so easy to cry these days.

I just had a visit from my old friend, Angela Lee, who was my classmate in law school. She was accompanied by her husband, Jeffrey. He was my classmate in Bartley Secondary School, where we both went for the first three months of Pre-University 1. Their visit brought me back to the time when we were in university, a time when we were reading law and Jeffrey was studying Arts & Social Sciences. It brought back memories that were both happy and sad. Happy moments because we spent some of the best years of our lives being carefree with no worries, just having fun. Feelings of sadness simply because when we look at ourselves now, we find how much we have aged, how ill I was and how things will not be the same ever again.

THIRTEEN

UNDERAGE SEX

I read in the newspapers that Spencer Gwee, a former high-flying DPP whom I defended for underage sex, lost his final appeal at the Court of Appeal. I defended him in the Subordinate Court.

It was very difficult to defend Spencer Gwee because he had his own way of thinking and he didn't care much about what my assistants Diana or Sunil had to say. He wanted to do everything himself and I had many disagreements with him. He even rejected the submission we had prepared and said that we had to submit his submission, not ours, because he had done a lot of research on it. We said, "It's your life, you know, and it's your fate. If you want to do it, so be it." So we submitted his submission. He was made to do a little bit of amendments here and there and it was finally completed. He was found guilty and the judge sentenced him to four months' imprisonment, which I thought was fair.

However, the next thing I knew, I was getting into a lot of problems with him regarding the appeal and the petition of appeal. So, I wrote a letter to him telling him that we wanted to discharge ourselves — and we did. We asked him to pay our fees. Even though he did not pay the full sum, he paid quite a substantial amount of it. We let it go because John Koh, a former DPP and a good friend of Spencer Gwee, was the one who recommended me to Spencer. So, for everybody's sake, I decided to just let it go.

Subsequently, he went to see a Senior Counsel, Chelva Rajah. I am not sure why Spencer chose Chelva to do this criminal appeal as he had not done much criminal law. I believe he would have his own reasons. Chelva Rajah went and argued before Justice Choo Han Teck, who was known for not writing his judgements, and if he did, for writing very short judgements. After hearing the case, Justice Choo dismissed the appeal on the basis that the judge was right in convicting Spencer Gwee. He wrote a concise judgement, explaining why he dismissed the appeal.

Chelva Rajah then put forward a further argument. They were not satisfied with Justice Choo's decision and applied to go to the Court of Appeal on a question of public interest, stating various reasons that they wanted to ask. When Diana got hold of the papers, she came to my office and we discussed the matter. I said, "I don't know what public interest they are talking about because as far as I am concerned, there is no public interest." Diana, who had practised for only two years, said, "It's so simple. They are just trying to see whether they can use the Court of Appeal as a back-door way of appealing." I laughed. True enough, when the case came to the Court of Appeal, it was not even allowed to take off because the Court of Appeal was of the view that there was no public interest involved. The Court of Appeal dismissed the appeal and ordered Spencer Gwee to start his prison sentence.

I was kind of sad that Spencer had to go to jail because however obnoxious or quarrelsome he may be, he is an intelligent person and also very kind hearted. I didn't think that he deserved to go to jail. I don't think any of these people who were involved in commercial sex should have been sent to jail because the punishment is much too harsh for the offence that they committed.

FOURTEEN

SPECIAL, IN EVERY SENSE
OF THE WORD

1993. "Papa, you are my friend, my partner and then my Papa." These words flashed through my mind one day at dialysis. It brought on a smile and so much pride remembering how it was said to me by my sweet little child, Sujesh, when he was three years old, but I also ached as I felt that I wouldn't be there for him much longer.

I am a proud father, like all fathers, and used to entertain a lot just to show him off. He was a precocious child who grew up hanging around adults and was comfortable with anyone he met; he always had a smile for everyone. He is the bond between Vimi and I, and he has acquired the best qualities from both of us.

I recollect his growing up years with so much fondness and love. Sometimes I regret that I was not able to indulge in sports activities with him like most fathers could but I made up for it by being a friend whom he could turn to in confidence. We shared a passion for soccer and enjoyed watching most matches together. There were the action movies we loved so much that we would borrow videos and watch reruns. I also made it a point to have dinner at home as often as I could as I loved to spend time with him. We don't share much casual conversations but he knows that I am always there for him. It shows when he would come to me when he is in doubt of a situation. The friend in me would step forward and I think he appreciates that.

Subhas and son, Sujesh, in a photo taken
on Subhas' birthday, 25 December 2006.

When he was four years old, he said that wanted to be a lawyer
when he grew up. I think it was simply because he was surrounded
by lawyers in the family. However, by the time he was a teenager
that desire to be a lawyer vanished for a while as he was keen on
mathematics. And then after completing his 'O' levels, and without
much consultation with us, he opted to pursue a Diploma in Banking
& Finance at a polytechnic, much to my disappointment at that time
as I still had the stereotypical mentality that everyone should go on to
do 'A' levels after completing their 'O' levels. So it was a little tough
for me to comprehend his decision but, as 'a good friend' would, I
supported it. However, after completing the diploma, he said that he
couldn't see himself pursuing a degree in finance.

One day, he told Vimi and I that he would read law. Deep within
me, I felt so pleased with his decision. He has all the qualities of a good
lawyer. But I did not wish to put pressure on him and so I smiled at
him and said, "Do whatever you want, son. Most importantly, you
must be passionate about your work to have a happy life. Otherwise, it
would be drudgery every day. My feet are smaller than yours. So don't

try to fit into my shoes! Wear your own shoes! But above all, be a good person."

I would very much wish to see Sujesh graduate in 2016. I wonder if I am asking for too much time. At the moment, I can only take each day as it comes. I am sitting here three times a week, dialysing — and I do feel trapped here. There is no chance of going abroad for his convocation. This is a very sad and miserable reality that I now face but I am glad that he will finally graduate.

Reflecting on a day in May 2014. My son has been making regular trips to Singapore from Nottingham, where he's reading law. Ever since I have been unwell, and whenever there is a short break in the university term, he would fly home to be with me and to keep me company. In every sense, he is special, for he is the only child I have.

Recently, after a month in Singapore for his Easter break, Sujesh had to return to his studies. I decided that I should see him off at the airport as I felt that it could be my last time with him. I told my wife to make it an outing. I was tired of staying at home and only going for dialysis and doing nothing else. She naturally agreed as she was trying to boost my spirits and found this a good opportunity to do something different for me. We went to the airport with our niece, Seeta, who often visited me. As I was still quite feeble to walk the long distance at the airport, Vimi decided to push me in the wheelchair. On hearing that I was making a trip out, Sunil, his wife, Sharon, and our niece, Sunita, were quite excited about it and joined us at the airport too.

After Sujesh had checked in, we had dinner in a restaurant nearby. It was very tiring for me but I did my best not to dampen the mood of those I love around me. We had a good dinner but then found out that Sujesh's flight had been delayed from midnight to 3:00 am because of

Vimi, Subhas and Sujesh eight years later, Christmas Eve, 2014.

technical problems. Already feeling so tired, I just couldn't wait with Sujesh any longer. He was unperturbed by the delay and called up his friends who lived in the east to join him and help him pass the time. It was already so late into the night and I was grateful that Sujesh had friends who care this much for him. One of those friends who agreed to meet him is a dear girl called Sabrina, who is a few years older than my son. She is always so obliging to him. I could see that she really cared for him like an older sister would.

After we had left the restaurant and were at the lobby saying our goodbyes, Sujesh turned to me, looking all grown up and strong, and gave me a hug and said, "Papa, I'll see you in one month's time when I come back in June."

Feeling very tired, weak and unsure of what tomorrow would bring, I said, "I will see you when I see you," as I held his hand. He just looked at me, holding back his emotions and walked away.

You see, I don't take things for granted anymore. I just cannot say that whatever I want will definitely happen. Who knows, with my condition, if I will be alive or not in one month's time? Those around me were emotionally shaken into reality that that was so true.

The poor boy had to wait the whole night as the flight was further delayed and only took off at 6:45 am. I was just glad that part of the time was spent with friends who cared for him.

Although Sujesh is reading law, there is a chance he may not want to practise it. He likes to keep his options open till later. I have told him that I have no objection to whatever he wants to do because that is his life. I have to accept certain decisions he makes. This past one-month vacation was for him to study and prepare for his first-year exams. I saw him studying very little, but then I can't say much because I, too, only studied at the last minute. He is a lot like me in many ways and I am confident he will do well in life as a good person.

The Anandan family, Chinese New Year, 2011.

FIFTEEN

OBSESSIVE LOVE

The case of Pathip Selvan s/o Sugumaran vs Public Prosecutor is a case that I would like to mention because there is a very important virtue from it that teenagers today must learn — tolerance.

Pathip Selvan s/o Sugumaran, otherwise known as Marsiling Baby because he lived in Marsiling, was going out with a girl named Jeevitha Panippan, a kindergarten teacher, for some time. He was crazily in love with her but the same thing could not be said of her. She flirted around and had other boyfriends, and she made use of Pathip whenever she wanted to. To make him jealous, sometimes she would ask him to go to her flat where she stayed with her father (her parents were divorced) and tell him to look through her window. He would do so only to see her sleeping with one of her other boyfriends.

Whenever Pathip went over to her flat, he would discover the truth, seeing a stranger in his girlfriend's room. There were many occasions when he threatened her with a knife, saying he would kill her. Each time he threatened her, she relented and apologized, and they would make up.

On one occasion, Pathip and Jeevitha had unprotected sex. She was troubled as she did not want to get pregnant. Pathip assured her that if she did get pregnant, he would marry her as he loved her. She was also afraid that he would abandon her even though Pathip assured her that if he did not love her, he would not have had sex with her. Despite his assurance and promise of marriage, she was still confused and made a complaint of rape to the police later that day.

That night, as he was nearing home, Pathip saw police officers in his house and decided not to enter in case they were looking for him. He called Kathik, their mutual friend, and asked him where his girlfriend was. He heard from Kathik that she had attempted suicide. Pathip decided not to return home until he found out what was going on.

A few days later, Pathip called his mother. She told him that his girlfriend had made a complaint to the police that Pathip had raped her. Pathip was desperate to reach her but could only do so through Kathik. He managed to speak to her then and when he asked her why she told the police he raped her, she broke down and cried. She said that she was confused and did not know why she had done that. She promised him that she would withdraw the complaint.

Subsequently, Pathip met with her father, Panippan, and informed him that he wanted to marry his daughter. "Out of curiosity, why do you want to marry my daughter suddenly?" Panippan asked. Pathip said that she was pregnant and had lodged a police report against him for raping her. All confused, Panippan said that he would discuss the matter with his daughter. The next day, she told Pathip over the telephone that she was unhappy that he had met with her father without her. She wanted him to surrender himself to the police, which he did the next day. He was released on bail and was warned not to see or talk to her until the case was concluded.

A few days later, she called Pathip to enquire how he was doing and informed him that she was going for a pregnancy test. She also said she would withdraw the complaint against him. After withdrawing the complaint, she went to Sentosa with him and spent the night there in a tent with him. She behaved as though everything was back to normal. After some time, she went back to the same routine again, provoking him by saying that she had other boyfriends and telling him to come to the flat and look through her bedroom window.

Pathip seriously wanted to marry her and was prepared to forgive her infidelity. They decided to try and settle things once more and he hoped to make her realise that what she was doing was wrong. So he made an appointment to see her. For some reason, he went to a shop and bought a sharp knife. He also bought her a Winnie the Pooh correction tape as a reconciliation gift. Initially he didn't explain to the police why he had bought her a gift but instead said he had never intended to use the knife because it was enough to threaten her with it as she would start crying and would ask for forgiveness. "And so, now I will forgive her and give her this gift and everything will be alright."

Pathip met Jeevitha at a coffee shop where she was sitting with her mother. Later he and Jeevitha took a walk to a park in Bishan area. He had planned to bring her to a secluded place to talk with her and threaten her. During the conversation she told him that the current boyfriend whom she was with and whom Pathip had seen, was a better lover than he was and a better man, too. This infuriated Pathip who, instead of just threatening her with the knife, stabbed her a number of times. He also snatched from her neck the chain that he had given her and fled to Johor Bahru.

From Johor Bahru he managed to call his mother, who went over to see him. He confessed to his mother what he had done. She asked him to return to Singapore but he didn't want to. She advised him that he could not live as a fugitive forever. He decided to take her advice and came back to Singapore where he was arrested and charged for the murder.

His family came to me because they lived in Marsiling and knew of me as I used to live in Sembawang. Marsiling was a part of Sembawang. It is quite common for people in Sembawang who get into serious trouble to come to me. The boy's parents asked me to help their son. They knew that their son had done something wrong but all they wanted was for him not to be hanged. They just wanted to try to save his life. I said, "We will do what we can but there is no guarantee." I do not know why but they went around telling everybody that I guaranteed that their son would not be hanged. That is something no lawyer should do — give guarantees.

Anyway, when Jeevitha's family came to know about this, they were very angry, thinking that Pathip was going to get off. They said that if he got off, they would take revenge and kill his sister. So it was getting a bit complicated and serious. Anyway, when I heard about it, I called his parents and told them to keep their mouths shut and not to say that I had given any guarantee when I had not told them so. I added that if they did not follow instructions, I would discharge myself from further acting for their son. They kept quiet after that.

I interviewed Pathip in prison. He said he was very sorry for what he had done and he was prepared to face whatever consequences because he had killed the only girl whom he ever loved. He was also prepared to face the death sentence because life now had no more meaning without her.

When I told his parents his wishes, they were upset that he had given up the fight.

The next time I saw him, he said he was remorseful, that he didn't want to die and he asked me to save his life. I assured him that I would do my best for him. I intended to use the sudden provocation argument, on the basis of the victim calling my client a lesser man and comparing him to other lovers. Under the law, this exchange amounted to sudden provocation, so we were quite confident we would be able to reduce the charge to culpable homicide. But the judge didn't agree with us. He said it was a murder and convicted my client for murder and sentenced him to death. Of course, we were not happy with the decision and we appealed to the Court of Appeal on the basis that the trial judge was wrong in convicting Pathip as he had not considered two defences raised in the lower court — provocation and diminished responsibility. The Court of Appeal held that there was sudden provocation and that Parthip was entitled to that defence though they dismissed the defence of diminished responsibility. Justice VK Rajah, in delivering his judgement put it that this was a tragic case of a young couple who had a bitter-sweet relationship that culminated in a homicide.

You see, when we talk about sudden provocation, the sudden provocation has to be so grave and sudden that the person would have lost control when he did the act — and this was exactly what happened to Pathip when his girlfriend told him that the person whom she was caught with by Pathip was a better lover than he was. That was considered words that could be hurting and provocative. But this also depends on the type of society we live in. In certain countries and in certain societies, those words may not be considered provocative because they are acceptable, but in Asian societies and especially where the cultures of the people are different, these words can be considered very damaging.

Pathip genuinely loved his girlfriend but she was fooling around and this was quite obvious from the facts of the case. She had many boyfriends and it was a fact that she was using Pathip as just another boyfriend from whom she can get things. She went too far before she realised that Pathip was angry. Instead of reconciling with him like she used to do before this incident, she blurted out that her other boyfriend was a better lover. In fact, I think she said something like, "He performed better in bed than you." Words of this nature are considered sufficient provocation.

You see, in this sort of matters, one should be careful with one's language because one does not know how the other party is going to react. There could be a guy who could say, "If he is a better lover than I am, stick with him. I have nothing more to do with you," and walk away. But then, there could be those who would react like Pathip. That is why I say that when parties are in a relationship, they should be very careful of what they say to each other because you do not know what would trigger off violence which could ultimately lead to death.

Pathip knew when he started his relationship with her that prior to him, she had 16 boyfriends. He was still prepared to have her as his girlfriend and to marry her. He even gave her a *thalli* (Hindu symbol of marriage) to profess his genuine love for her. He claimed that he did not care what she did in her past; what was important was the present and the future but obviously she was not on the same wavelength. She was thinking of having more and more fun and even when she was with Pathip, accepting his gifts, she was seeing other boys. In some sense she was asking for trouble.

On the day of the confrontation when Pathip pulled her behind the power station where the offence took place, and demanded to know "who was the man in the red shirt who was in bed with you this morning", she was stunned that he had found out and she told him in Tamil, "He's better than you in bed. That is why I am interested in him." That was when Pathip took the knife and stabbed her. After stabbing her, he knelt down to kiss her on the right cheek before pulling off the *thalli* from around her neck. To him, it was exactly what it was — a matrimonial symbol of marriage — and that she was his wife. He threw the *thalli* aside and walked off. He said he had never been so sad when he heard what she said.

The Court of Appeal agreed with us and wanted to give Pathip life imprisonment. My nephew Sunil, who was there for the sentencing hearing (as I was in hospital), argued for ten years' imprisonment and said that life imprisonment was too strict and should not be given. Subsequently, the Court of Appeal partially agreed with Sunil and handed down a sentence of 20 years' imprisonment. This meant he would be out in around 13 years. Since Pathip was in his 20s, he still had a life to look forward to. I hope that he has learnt his lesson in prison. He would have a lot of time to reflect on what it was that was wrong.

Sometimes, I wonder why one has to do something so drastic as to kill a girl. If a girl doesn't like you or if she compares you to somebody else, the best thing to do is to walk away. There are many girls who deserve your love. Go and find somebody else instead of getting into trouble.

SIXTEEN

MY DEAR FRIEND, FRANCIS

Francis Yeo was one of my best friends at university. We were admitted the same year, in 1966. He studied Business Administration and I read Law. He was short and did not look impressive. He would come down to play football on the campus field. I realised how determined he could be though. He was a tough player, competitive and very brave, not at all afraid to tackle people much bigger in size. I noticed the way he played and I said, "This guy. Don't let his looks deceive you. He has a very strong character."

True enough we became friends on the football field and once in a while when he met me in the Union House, he would have coffee with me and we became good friends. Subsequently, we realised that we shared the same sentiment towards the political situation in Singapore. We were young and very idealistic. We were always critical and trying our best to expose the establishment for what we thought they were; at least we thought we were doing our part in trying to save Singapore from a dictatorship.

Francis Yeo was a generous person. He had a scholarship and when he had excess money from the scholarship fund, he would spend it on all his friends. He was always there if we needed a handout. He never hesitated to give his money but, of course, he would dispense a piece of advice, too. Many a time he told me that I spent too much money, especially on girls. He said that I should be more careful but he still gave me money. We became very close when we went to support *The Singapore Herald*, a newspaper run by a Malaysian whom the Prime Minister of Singapore thought was there to sabotage Singapore and wanted to ban the newspaper. Jimmy Han, the Managing Editor of the newspaper was facing an uphill task fighting the People's Action Party for its existence.

Francis Yeo, Sunny Chew, Sim Yong Chan, Danny Choo, Conrad Raj, Violet Oon and I went to help Jimmy Han along with many other university students. There was even talk at one time that Francis Yeo was going to take over the newspaper and that he was going to betray everybody else. But that was not true. I would trust Francis with my life. I would not expect him to betray anybody. Subsequently, despite all our efforts, the newspaper was closed. We all went our different ways. Francis went into business, Sunny Chew started his business as a company director and I went on to practise law.

At one stage, Francis Yeo went into the business with Sunny Chew. He injected money into Sunny's warehousing services company to expand it, and friends like Leonard Cheng also came in to help. As good friends would be good friends, we trusted Sunny Chew to manage the business which was doing very well. Unfortunately, Sunny did not pay enough attention to the company. He was more interested in playing the share market. In the end, we had to sell out. Though we didn't lose money, we did not make the type of profit we could have made.

Francis was a kind and generous person. He was always trusting as a person and inevitably got taken for a ride by some of his partners in Malaysia who deserted him and left him to face the debts. He was disillusioned with doing business with friends and decided to work for the church. In his later years, he discovered he was plagued with the dreaded disease — cancer.

It was very disturbing to know that Francis was sick with a life-threatening disease. There was not much I could do as a friend but to stand by him whenever he needed me. I visited him once or twice but he didn't seem to be keen on having visitors. He seemed distant and he was not the Francis Yeo I used to know. I felt helpless and wanted so much to make him happy.

Quite often our mutual friend, Jill Kuok and her husband, Sandford Friedman, would come to Singapore from Hawaii to visit with their son and his family. Sometimes, Sandford and I would hang out for a drink at a nightclub owned by one of my clients. When I suggested asking Francis along with us on one of those outings, both Jill and Vimi thought that it was a good idea because they knew that they could trust us to look after Francis well. I decided to also invite Sim Yong Chan and Conrad Raj. To my surprise, Francis was very keen to come along.

All five of us went, had drinks, reminisced about the old days and sang old, bawdy university songs that we loved and shared. Francis was in top form in everything we did but he got tired and had to leave a bit earlier. We stood up and he hugged me and said, "Thanks for the lovely night. I will never forget this night." With a heavy heart, knowing how sick my dear friend was, I said, "Francis, it doesn't have to be the last night. We can always make it happen and create more memories." With deep sadness in his eyes, he said, "I know."

Two weeks later, I called him to arrange another outing. He told me that he would like to go out again but he was undergoing chemotherapy and that made him very tired. He said that as soon as he'd finished the course and was feeling better, he would call me to have one more drink. Feeling very troubled as I felt that I would not see my friend again, I said, "Sure, I'll wait for your phone call."

A few days' later, I had a phone call from Sim Yong Chan telling me that Francis' son had called to say that Francis had passed away. Although I knew how sick Francis was, it was still a shock to hear of his passing. I had been looking forward to spending more time with him after his chemotherapy. I had to take it as another blow in my lifetime. It shattered me. So many beautiful memories flooded my mind and I couldn't hold back my tears for a dear beloved friend. Francis Yeo played an important part in my life especially during our university days. There was nothing I could do.

I went early in the morning with Sim Yong Chan to the chapel where his body was lying. With an aching heart, I looked at him, prayed for his soul and left. I never went back there for the evening wake, neither did I attend the funeral because I knew that I would not be able to take it. I didn't want to break down and cry in front of so many people. To me, Francis Yeo will always be an inspiration. A man full of courage, determination and, foremost of all, passion for his fellow human beings. I wish that there were more Francis Yeos in this world.

Throughout my career as a practising lawyer, spanning more than 40 years, I have come across many types of people, so much so that nothing surprises me anymore. Whatever you have to tell me about a certain event, I will not be surprised because I have seen how people behave and the things they do for their personal agendas.

I have come across many crooks, many conmen, many vicious people who find it easy to inflict pain — some near-death — on others. But some of the biggest crooks are the lawyers themselves!

I say this with great regret because ours is supposed to be a very noble profession. But there are lawyers who have destroyed for their own personal gain, lawyers who have run away with clients' money, lawyers who have cheated their clients by telling them lies, and lawyers who have forged documents to convince clients that they are doing their work. The worst was the lawyer who took money from a poor old widow, ran away with it and spent it on gambling, leaving this poor lady in a very hopeless plight. Then there are the lawyers who won't take anybody's money, who won't cheat you but would pretend to be noble and do a lot of pro bono work not for the sake of the accused person but for the sake of their own publicity. They are not genuine people.

Pro bono has been abused as a cover and I detest those who do that because pro bono is such a noble thing to do.

I have done a lot of pro bono work from the time I started my practice, never boasted about it, never got much publicity out of it. But every time when I see some people being interviewed regarding their pro bono work, I laugh because even the Government is coming into the picture. They had considered forcing all lawyers to do pro bono work. Pro bono is something that comes from your heart. You should have the desire to help. It should not be forced upon you. The authorities don't realise this. The moment you force pro bono on lawyers, you take away the meaning of pro bono. Those who are genuinely concerned and do pro bono also will be classified as people who have to do it because they have been told to do so.

SEVENTEEN

HOW I STARTED PRACTICE

Some time in 1970, my family had to move from the British Naval Base because my father stopped working for the British Government. We moved into Kampong Wak Hassan, a Malay village where we bought a house to stay.

Before my father retired, his boss said to him, "I don't know why you want to stay in that place when your daughter is a doctor and your son is a lawyer. It's not right for you to stay there." My father who was more concerned about collecting his salary and bonus, said, "Fair enough, but what about my salary? According to the contract, you have to give me one more month of salary?" His boss said "No," without explaining further.

Anyway, we had already decided we would leave and so, we left the Base. We settled down in a single storey bungalow on Temporary Occupation Licence land in Kampong Wak Hassan, surrounded by Malays. We made a lot of new Malay friends. Our immediate neighbour was an Indian family.

One of the first things I did when I became a lawyer was to engage the British authorities. I wanted them to pay my father the one-month's salary due to him. I received a response from Drew & Napier telling me that they were taking instructions. Later, they rang me up and said, "What if we don't pay? Who are you going to sue? Do you know it's not easy to sue the British Government under the Crown Proceedings Act?" I said, "I will find a way to help my father. Besides, it's not fair to cheat my father of his S$360, which was his monthly salary. I think, after sacrificing so many years for the British, this is not the way to say goodbye. He should not be cheated of his dues."

Even if I were to lose the case, it didn't matter. The public would be able to see what sort of an employer the British Government was. After about two weeks, I received a cheque for $360 issued to my father. I handed the cheque promptly to him. He was so pleased. He wanted to keep the cheque as a souvenir but later decided to cash it after taking a photocopy of it. When his friends learnt that we managed to recover the money, they wanted me to help them to recover theirs as well. I said, "No, I think my father is lucky because the lawyer from Drew & Napier seems to be an understanding man and he realised that the person is my father. I don't think I will be able to succeed for you people." As it would be, they engaged other lawyers who wrote to the British authorities. Drew & Napier replied on their instructions to act. Regrettably, they informed my father's friends that the British Government was not paying anything.

For my father, this was a sweet victory even though the amount was small. He went around the neighbourhood, proudly sharing with friends, "Look, my son, the lawyer, got this money for me. He has taken on the big British Crown. They were scared." He added a lot of spice to his story.

To process the title deed to the Kampong Wak Hassan house, my father engaged the services of a lawyer called MPD Nair, formerly a minister in the Lim Yew Hock cabinet. He was then the lawyer for most Malayalees in Singapore. My father told me to see him. "Can you go down to town? Please see this lawyer, Mr MPD Nair, to collect the title deed because the lawyer has been sending us letters." Naturally, I agreed to do so. I went to Mr MPD Nair's office which was in Winchester House on Collyer Quay. It was a very dingy old building but there were many law firms there.

He came out of his office and asked me, "Are you the son who is the lawyer, who has just been called to the Bar?" I replied, "Yes." He seemed very pleased and said, "Please come in, please come in." So I went into his room and while I had a cup of coffee, he asked me what my plans were. I replied, "I do not know. I've already got a place in Cooper Brothers to do my Chartered Accountancy and I am just toying with the idea whether I should or should not take it." He said, "Well, it looks like a very good combination but it's a tough course. I do not know whether you will able to stay in England without being homesick?" With that, we both laughed.

He told me, "Look, if you ever need a place to practise, come to my office." As he pointed across his room, he added, "I have an empty desk over there. You can start a small practice from here." I thanked him for his offer and went back with the title deed.

Coincidentally, my friend, SK Ho, got into trouble with the authorities for vandalism and that was my first case. I needed to apply for my practising certificate and I needed an office. So I went to see Mr Nair and told him, "Sir, I may need your premises for a little while because my friend is in trouble and I am engaged to defend him." Happily he replied, "The offer is still open. The desk is over there. You can sit in the same room as me and do whatever you want to do." I said, "OK," and thanked him.

In 1971, I started my firm "Subhas Anandan, Advocate & Solicitor" from Mr Nair's premises. His firm was known as MPD Nair, Advocate & Solicitor. He did not want to take any rent from me. All he said was, "Just pay for your own telephone." I was a bit surprised because lawyers are known to charge even their own colleagues for anything. Mr MPD Nair (Mr Nair, as I respectfully referred to him) said to me, "I do not want to take anything from you. I just want to wish you well. Stay here as long as you want."

As my practice improved, I forgot the idea of going to London to do Chartered Accountancy. I remained on the premises and became quite close to Mr Nair. I found him an exceptional man, who was not proud as a man or as a lawyer. He was honest and compassionate. In many ways, he was very kind and many people took advantage of his kindness. I remember one particular incident when a man approached him for money to buy a coffin for his deceased mother. The same man did that to him three times and each time his response to me was, "We must always give the other person the benefit of the doubt. This could really be the actual situation now."

I learnt a lot from him, most particularly, understanding how people think. This is a man who was once a Cabinet minister and today, he's sitting in a dingy old office, still practising law with a compassion that so far I have not seen in anybody. Not only did he become a dear friend, he became a sort of mentor; whenever I asked him something which I am not familiar with, he would do his best to help me.

In late January 1976, when I was wrongfully arrested and detained, Mr Nair often came to see me in prison. He was the only person whom I had to console while everybody else came to console me. This was because, whenever Mr Nair came, I would always see his eyes glistening with tears. He would always tell me, "This is not right. What they are doing to you is not right." I would reply, "What can we do Mr Nair? We've got to accept all that is happening." Then I would shake his hand each time. Sometimes he would sit there for ten to

Mr MPD Nair at his office in International Plaza, Anson Road.
The photograph on the right was taken two weeks before he passed
away suddenly on 15 January 1989.

20 minutes, just looking at me. He felt helpless and each time as he got
up to leave, I would always tell him, "You are a busy man, Mr Nair.
You don't have to come any more." He would always insist, "No, no,
no, I will always come and visit you." I thought, "This is a man whom
I met by chance because of some title deed and now he has become so
close to me."

When I was released from prison in mid-November 1976, I went
back to the office. He asked me what my plans were. I said to him, "I
really do not know what my plans are, Mr Nair, as I am so confused
that I don't know what to do." But I knew one thing for sure. I would
fight this government and this oppressive law. I had noticed while in
prison, laws had been abused by the police and others in authority. He
looked at me and said, "Don't get into any further trouble." I assured
him, "Yes, I will not."

He looked at me again and asked if I would like to be his partner.
I said, "Mr Nair, everybody is shunning me like an untouchable because

of the stigma of having been to prison and being known as the anti-establishment man and you are offering me partnership? Are you sure you know what you are talking about?" Reassuringly, he replied, "I am sure." He said, "I know who you are. The few years that you have been here, I know your character. I am making this offer very sincerely."

Feeling quite pleased, I asked him, "What is the percentage going to be as your partner?" He replied, "50-50."

With a smile on my face, I exclaimed, "That's fair enough!" He said he would change the name to MPD Nair & Subhas Anandan. I rejected the offer of the name and instead suggested to rename it MPD Nair & Co. I also told him that even though we were 50-50 partners, I didn't mind him taking a little bit more of the profit because he was married and had three children while I was a happy-go-lucky bachelor who didn't need much money. He was touched by my gesture and said, "We'll see."

In time, the partnership became stronger with greater trust and understanding. Eventually, I brought more partners into the firm. Mr Nair however felt that he was not pulling his weight as he was getting old and his clients were not really very significant people. I said to him, "Please don't do anything rash. You are still going to be a senior partner and you will remain in this firm." I managed to convince him that he was very useful to the image of the firm. He agreed and we went on as partners till the day he passed away suddenly in January 1989.

In the process of meeting him, I met his father-in-law, Mr VK Nair, a very enterprising man. I also got to meet Mr MPD Nair's sister-in-law, Vimala, whom I married later and became a part of their big happy family of 11 siblings. Two of Mr MPD Nair's three children read law. Both of them did their internship and pupilage under me.

Like their father, his two children who did law were quite reliable where work was concerned.

In all my years of practice, I have yet to find someone able to match up to Mr MPD Nair, who was kind and compassionate. We shared the same values and sentiments in the way we practised law. I feel that I have done my duty by passing on his values in practice to his son, Kesavan (Kesi), who was eager to learn the ways of his father's style of practice. He is now doing well for himself.

When Mr Nair died, I was already married to Vimi and we were staying in the same neighbourhood, just two blocks from each other. On that fateful day, we received a phone call and rushed to his home. Sadly, he was already gone by the time we got there. He had difficulty breathing that morning which led to a heart attack. I was at a loss; I didn't know what to do.

Suddenly I was head of the firm, with lawyers and staff to worry about. I also had to think about Mr Nair's family and I tried my best to keep the firm that carried his name going in the hope that some day his children could take over the legacy he left behind. But sadly, it was not meant to be as I was falling ill and his children were still young in practice and were unable to keep the firm.

EIGHTEEN

MPD NAIR, JBJ AND THE NCMP SCHEME

Mr MPD Nair was Minister for Communications and Works in the Lim Yew Hock government. When the PAP government took over in 1959, he left for London to read law. After Mr Nair returned from London, he started his practice immediately in 1963. Politics was still in his blood. He joined the Workers' Party where JB Jeyaretnam (JBJ) was Secretary-General.

In one particular deposition, sometime in the 1970s, JBJ and I were jointly representing the defendants — he for one party and I for the other. Howard Cashin was for the plaintiff. JBJ called a few lawyers as his witnesses and after he had finished cross-examining them, it was my turn. My cross-examination of these witnesses was much more effective in bringing out the truth. In fact, one of the lawyers who was himself a witness came back the next day and said, "You know, Mr. Anandan, I went back and thought about what you said and I think you are right. Maybe what I said in court was not right." It took a great man to admit that he could have made a mistake, and that man was Mr C Arul. We became very close friends after the case. He invited me for lunch to tell me how much he appreciated the way I cross-examined him. Eventually, the case was settled.

Years later, JBJ was charged for criminal offences. He told Mr Nair that he was going to engage a Queen's Counsel (QC) from London to defend him. In the meantime, he wanted Mr Nair to speak with me and to ask me to defend him and hold the fort. Mr Nair asked him, "Why? He is so young and you have so many older lawyers in your Party." He replied, "I know, but I am impressed with him and want him to become my defence counsel."

So Mr Nair told me that he wanted me to defend his friend, JBJ. I said "No, don't get me involved. This is going to be very complicated and consequences can be very drastic. I don't think I want to get involved."

But Mr Nair was faithful to his friend and would not take no for an answer. Every day he would come and leave on my desk authorities, cases that he researched for me to read for the defence of JBJ. Papers were piling up.

One day, I walked over to his room and said, "Mr Nair, what is it that you want me to do? You have cluttered my table with all your authorities, some relevant, some not relevant. What is it you want me to do?" He replied, "Subhas, this man needs to be defended. He is my friend. He is the Secretary-General of the Party. I am his bailor. He wants you to defend him and I said you would. So can you look at it as helping me?"

Hearing his request in that manner, I couldn't say no to him. I said, "OK, I will, on one condition. Please stop putting authorities on my table." He laughed and said, "Alright, Subhas. Thank you." That was how I got involved with JBJ.

JBJ engaged John Mortimer QC, with whom I got along very well. Because of the case, I also met Martin Thomas QC, Baron Hugh Emlyn Hooson QC and Louis Blom-Cooper QC. The memorable experience of meeting all these great men cannot be compared with anything else. It only fanned my desire to become a better litigator.

Subhas with John Mortimer QC at the office
he shared with MPD Nair.

Whenever it was possible, Mr Nair would come to court to give us encouragement. He would sit at the back of the courtroom. In the end, JBJ won but it was a shallow victory because he was not given a pardon. He was still out of the Assembly, still out of Parliament.

In the 1984 general election, the government introduced a new scheme called a Non-Constituency Member of Parliament (NCMP), which simply entitled the candidate who was defeated by the narrowest margins to be given a place in Parliament. Mr Nair, who stood in Jalan Kayu, was the closest defeated candidate. He lost to his opponent by about 500 votes. So he was given the invitation to join the Parliament and he was very excited.

He told me, "Subhas, the whole country is my constituency! I will speak for everybody." However, JBJ came up and told him that the Executive Committee had met and had decided that he should not accept the position because they were against the introduction of the NCMP Scheme. JBJ said, "We will stick to our principle and you will not accept this."

I could actually see the heartbreak in Mr Nair's face. He told me, "Subhas, they told me that I can't take it." I was so upset for Mr Nair. I said, "Why don't you ask the Party to go to hell!" He said, "I can't do that."

So I rang up JBJ and said, "Why are you not allowing him to do this?" He gave me a long story. I was not convinced. When the newspapers interviewed me, I said it was very unfair that my partner, MPD Nair, was not allowed to accept the NCMP post. But Mr Nair was an honourable man. He abided by the decision of the Workers' Party Council and rejected the offer of NCMP.

In years to come after that, in the 1997 general election, JBJ was the closest defeated candidate. He was given the same offer which he accepted. I telephoned JBJ to ask why he was accepting it. "Isn't it your Party's decision not to accept this sort of invitation? You stopped MPD Nair from taking it?" I asked curiously. He said, "Well, Subhas, circumstances change. The Council feels that I must accept it," came his reply. I just shook my head and said to myself, "This is the most unfair situation." Anyway, it was a political decision that had nothing to do with me.

NINETEEN

FEELING USEFUL

It is now June 2014. It has been more than six months since I was treated by Dr Ching Chi Keong. I seem to be feeling a lot stronger, emotionally and physically. I am able to walk a longer distance and even climb steps in our condominium garden. Vimi would make me handle two steps at a time, pause for a long while, and then continue. It would seem like a great achievement after reaching the top of the steps. The motivation would always be to sit on the swing in the garden with Vimi for a while.

I am using a new dictaphone. I am not familiar with it but it will be easier for Vimi to transcribe.

Today I had two visitors at home. One is a very close and dear friend, Christopher Woo. He had a client in Malaysia who was in trouble and Chris wanted me to get involved in the case and to assist in certain aspects of it. I met Chris Woo when I was a consultant in Harry Elias Partnership (HEP) in 2000. I also met Lawrence Quahe when they were both partners in HEP. Both of them subsequently left HEP — Chris Woo to Rajah & Tann, and Lawrence Quahe to join his client, a big Indonesian tobacco company. After a few years, they got together to start a legal practice called Lawrence Quahe & Woo.

Lawrence was a good boss. Several legal assistants left HEP to join him in his new firm. Lawrence and Chris also visited me to invite me to join them. They said it didn't matter if I was not able to 'pull my weight in numbers' but they would like me to join them. However, I was not in a position to do so because RHT Law was then depending on me to head the litigation department, and I did not want it to seem as though I was betraying them. When I explained this to Lawrence and Chris, they said, "Look here, Subhas, anytime when you need to leave, please remember that there is a room for you here." Feeling rather pleased with them, I replied, "That's very reassuring. Thank you very much."

Subsequently, Michael Palmer, another partner from HEP, joined Lawrence and Chris. I often refered to the three of them affectionately as "The Boys". I really thought that Lawrence Quahe and Chris Woo were great people, especially when they stood loyal to their old buddy, Michael.

The Boys and I used to enjoy lunches together, talking and laughing. When I fell really ill, and I was not sure what my future was going to be like, they visited me in hospital to reassure me that everything was going to be alright. They would say, "When you come out and if there is anything that you feel you need to change, or if you feel that you are not wanted, we still want you. Remember that the room that we promised you in 2011 is still there. You can come there with your team and join us. It doesn't matter whether you have heart failure or kidney failure. We are your friends and we will always stand by you." I was very touched and I controlled my tears but as soon as they left the room, I broke down. I didn't want them to see me cry.

Soon after I was discharged from hospital and recuperating at home, still quite sick but not as bad as when I was in hospital, they came again with the other partners. They brought lunch and Lawrence told me the same thing. "Remember the offer that we made, it's always there for you. We shall not repeat it. You just have to make one phone call and we will come and take all your things and put you in our place. We'll always be there for you."

As I said at the beginning of this chapter, Chris Woo came to my home with a client. He said, "Initially, I was not happy to get you involved but your nephew, Sunil, says that you are going back to the office two to three hours on

Subhas with The Boys. From left: Lawrence Quahe, Chris Woo and Michael Palmer.

non-dialysis days. This is why I decided to come and see you. I don't want you to tax yourself. If you are tired, you are tired, and there is no going the extra mile at the expense of your health." I smiled at his caring ways and said, "OK." He said he had given us another two cases which Sunil was handling for the time being. He said, "When you get better and you feel up to it, you will take over."

We had a good meeting this morning and once again, I felt useful. I think my life is slowly going back to normal and I think I have to accept the fact that though there are limitations to what I can now do because of my dialysis, life goes on and I have got to be strong for my family and friends. I intend to do that.

TWENTY

AH SOO,
A DEAR OLD FRIEND

My friend, Wong Ah Soo, is a very dear friend who grew up with me in the British Naval Base. We shared an adventurous childhood, always up to mischief and pranks and we loved every minute of it. In the Base there were apartment blocks reserved for families and others reserved for bachelors. Block 47 was one of the bachelors' quarters. Ah Soo always said that he and I would not have girlfriends, would not get married and we would live in Block 47 Room 2 as each room could be occupied by two persons. I would always agree with him and said that we would have a good time sharing the room. Years passed and we parted company. He went on to work and I went on to university to read law. I got married and he did not.

Ah Soo is now in a very bad shape. He is suffering from the initial stages of dementia. He can't recognise people sometimes and sometimes he doesn't know what he is saying. He would forget a situation that happened five minutes ago.

Sometime in 2010, I had a call from his sister, Mabel, a very lovely lady, and she told me, "Subhas, you have got to help me. Ah Soo is now suffering from dementia. He is giving a lot of problems. He would sit in the coffee shop and spend his money recklessly and lose his mobile phone. I wish you could talk to him." Definitely, I said, and asked for his telephone number.

I immediately called him and said, "Ah Soo, this is Subhas." He was pleasantly surprised and exclaimed, "Ah, it's so nice to hear your voice. Who gave you this number?" I explained that his sister had called me and we had chatted about him. He said to me, "Subhas, she must have told you that I was sick." Tactfully, I replied, "Well, she didn't say you were sick. She just told me that sometimes you need help. So, Ah Soo, tell me where are you staying now so that I can visit you and maybe we can go out for dinner?" He replied, "Are you sick or what?" Surprised at his question, I asked him, "Why do you ask?" He exclaimed, "I am in Block 47 Room 2 and we are staying together. What's wrong with you?"

I thought, "What his sister said is true!" I played along and said to him, "So sorry, sometimes I forget. Anyway, I have another house where I am staying and I have decided to give a dinner for all our old friends like Ah Teng, Ramli, Chee Kok and a few others. I think you should come." He was all excited and said, "Sure, I would love to come but I need someone to take me there." I assured him that I would make arrangements with Ramli to pick him up. I told him, "Oh by the way, Ah Soo, I am married, you know, and I have a son." He was very pleased but a little puzzled. He asked, "Then who has been living with me in Block 47 Room 2?" I told him I did not know and that Block 47 Room 2 does not exist any more. "I believe you are now staying somewhere in Toa Payoh." He said, "Times have changed and I can't cope sometimes but please call me and tell me when and ask Ramli to pick me up."

As it was Deepavali of 2010, I decided to invite my close childhood friends to my home for dinner. Vimi cooked a curry feast that they all liked. My siblings also knew Ah Soo very well as he used to hang out at our home quite often when we lived as neighbours in the British Naval

Base. They, too, were at my home that Deepavali for dinner. As agreed, Ramli picked up Ah Soo before coming over.

I had not seen Ah Soo for many years. He was an exact replica of his father and he hugged me and said, "You played me out, ah, by getting married."

I laughed and replied, "Well it was one of those things." I introduced him to Vimi, whom he seemed to have forgotten although he had met her many years ago, and he said to her, "He's supposed to stay with me as a bachelor in Block 47 Room 2 but obviously the situation has changed."

He seemed to be very lucid at times and knew what he was talking about. We all sat, chatted, reminisced about the good old days, ate and drank merrily. He was talking so sensibly. We reminisced about the days when we got up to all sorts of mischief. It was a great reunion of neighbours and friends whom we had not seen for many years but had always kept fondly in our thoughts. We talked about old times and there was no trace of Ah Soo's declining health.

Finally at around midnight, Ah Soo said he was tired and Ramli decided to take him home. In fact, as he was going back, he asked me, "When are we having the next one?" I said I would try to organise another one as soon as possible. Maybe we could organise a bigger one where we could call more friends. He said that would be a good idea.

A few days later, his sister rang and thanked me. She said, "I believe Ah Soo had a good time as he was only talking about the dinner and you. He seems to be quite OK now." I was pleased to hear that and assured her, "Any time there is a problem, please give me a call. Let me know what I can do for you."

A few days later she rang me up again. "Subhas, he is back to his abnormal self. He was running around the block at night, shouting out

A gathering of old friends, Deepavali 2010. Seated from left: Ah Teng, Subhas, Ah Soo and Molak. Standing are Ah Sai, Sai Chee, Kok Meng and Ramli.

your name and asking where you were." She said he was asking loudly, "Why are you leaving me alone?" The police had to control him and Mabel had to explain to them that he was not well, or he would have been charged for disorderly behaviour. We took him back home. Mabel was anxious and frantically asked me, "Can you do something about it?" I said, "OK, I will arrange for another dinner or we can visit him at the coffee shop that he normally visits." She was pleased that I would do that for her brother. I went looking for him at the coffee shop with Ramli but we did not see him there. We asked the shopkeeper and he confirmed that Ah Soo had not been there for two or three days. I called Mabel to tell her that we were not able to get in touch with Ah Soo to talk with him. She said that the family themselves did not know where he was. I thought the matter ended there.

A few weeks later, Mabel rang me and said that his condition had become worse. He couldn't even recognise anyone and they had to apply to court to have him committed and to apply for a committee to be set up to look after his interests because he was unable to look after himself. When I heard that, I was very sad. So many thoughts came flooding back. I thought about the memories of our childhood, our growing up years, the bond that we shared. I felt that I could not see him in that state.

Mabel rang me again and asked if I could provide an affidavit. The lawyers acting for the family wanted an affidavit giving the background of Wong Ah Soo and his relationship with his family and how they would treat him. Of course, I gave an affidavit that was favourable to his siblings. But I gave it with a very heavy heart. So many memories flooded back. It took me a long time to come to terms with his condition. I held back my tears because Ah Soo was one of my closest childhood friends and to see him in this state was heart-breaking. I informed his sister that even though I was sad, I would like to visit with him when she took him home. She said she would let me know when. But she has not called me yet. The day will come when she will call and I will go and see my good friend. I hope that he can recognise me. If he can't, it doesn't matter; but if he does, it matters a lot to me.

I realised then that when he was with friends, he seemed to be a different person altogether. He managed to carry on a conversation reasonably well.

Mabel has called. She shared with me that "he was running around the housing estate where he is living, shouting out your name and asking when is the party." She said he kept running and repeating himself and said that I was suppose to organise one soon. Mabel said to me,

"Were you supposed to do that? If so, I think you'd better not. He has definitely lost it. He can't hold himself well now. I don't think it would be safe to have him over."

On hearing this, my heart sank and I felt as though I have lost a dear friend although he was still physically around.

I waited a little while to call him. Many a time I called him to talk but sadly, he didn't seem to recognise my voice. Each time as I dialled, I wished to God that he would recognise my voice the moment I said, "Hello, Ah Soo,"

With Mabel Wong.

but he didn't. In fact, he seemed like a stranger who was rude, abrupt and wanted to hang up immediately as if I was a wrong caller. It was heart-wrenching to come to terms with his condition. I shared this with Mabel. She said, "This has been his pattern for some time."

I prayed for my friend to get better but he never got better and today, while at dialysis, Mabel walked in. She had heard from Ramli that I had to undergo dialysis and she came looking for me. She held my hand and said, "I never expected to see you like this but I have come to learn to expect the unexpected. I have been looking out for my brother for some time. During his lucid moments, he talks to me and he always talks about you. He tells me what a good friend and a great guy you are and how proud he is to know that he is your friend. He said even his photograph appeared with you in your book." It was one of the greatest satisfactions he had. I am so glad that I made him proud to be my friend.

Wong Ah Soo is truly a good friend. We grew up together and sometimes, we even shared the same plate of food. He cooked for us quite often, taking his mother's lap cheong (Chinese sausage) and other ingredients necessary to make a sumptuous meal of fried rice. We played hard together. He will never let me down in any sort of situation. Ah Soo is that sort of person who will give his life for his friends. This is why, sometimes, I think that once upon a time, I was the richest man in the world for I had friends who would go with me to the end of the world. Today friendship means so little to many people. It has become shallow for most. It has become a convenience. I make new friends and I know new friends are nothing compared to the old. This is how it is. Situations change and you have to learn how to adapt to these changes. If not, you will be a miserable man. Having said that, I do have some new friends who have become very close and dear to me.

TWENTY-ONE

SAD OCCASIONS AND HAPPY MOMENTS

Thinking about Wong Ah Soo brings me back again to the British Naval Base where I had spent my whole childhood. To most of us, it was the happiest time of our lives — simple carefree lives with little worry. It was fun most of the time. We all studied in the same school, some of us were in the same class, some of us were in the same level but in different classes. There was a sort of solidarity in our school that I have never known anywhere else.

Our school was not noted for its academic achievements because most of the students were not really interested in achieving academically. They just wanted to pass their Secondary 3 or Secondary 4 exams so that they could find a job and support their family or support themselves. Of course the school never discouraged anyone who wanted to study. I was the only one in my cohort who went to Raffles Institution and then to Singapore University to read law. I was given all the encouragement, not only by my friends and teachers but by parents who would turn around as I walk pass and say to their children, "Look, look at Subhas. Why don't you all be like him?"

I became some sort of a role model for the other children because I was good in sports and studies. I played many games but football was always my favourite. Employees within the Base had their own Football League. Asian 11 was first organised for those who had been rejected and who did not qualify to play for their own departments because they were not good enough. So all the rejected players started to play for Asian 11 and every other team who played against them would score ten to 13 goals simply because Asian 11 players were not used to playing the game. So the suggestion to allow the children of the employees to play came about. This idea was carried through, and soon my brother Sudheesh, Quah Kim Song and I joined the team. Kim Song's brother, Kim Siak, joined as the Captain of Asian 11 because there wasn't a football team in his department. In fact he was the one who recruited us to play for Asian 11.

Suddenly Asian 11 became a very powerful team. Some of those who had come to watch us play immediately arranged for us to have proper jerseys because we were wearing just singlets. We even had matching shorts and socks. Suddenly we were a team to be reckoned with. We won the league title and Kim Siak proudly received the Cup on behalf of the team. A big celebration was held after that.

Quah Kim Siak came from the famous footballing family of Quahs. I have had the privilege of playing with Kim Lai, Kim Swee and Kim Siak although I was younger than them. I know their standard of play and I would consider Kim Siak as the best of the Quah siblings in football. He retired from football and when he retired from work, he started a pub. We used to go there once in a while to patronise the pub. One day I noted that that Kim Siak was not well. I asked him, "How are you? Are you OK?" He would say, "Coming from you asking whether I am OK, it's funny. He laughed and added, "I should be asking you, are you OK?"

When I was in hospital fighting for my life, I was told that Kim Siak had died. I was very upset and regretted that I was not even in a position to attend his funeral. I felt miserable as once again, I was unable to attend the funeral of another dear friend because of my own ill health. At times like this, I would question, "Why is God so unkind to me? At least He should let me go and pay my last respects."

Kim Siak was somebody who loved his life, who loved having fun. I would like to think that in some way, I was a part of his life too. I reminisced about all the good times we had. We were neighbours and we were football mates. God bless his soul.

As I narrate these incidents, I do not know why most of the time it's the tragic events that come into play. One remembers sad occasions and it seems as though there are no happy moments.

This is not true. Underneath all that sadness, there are still happy moments.

TWENTY-TWO

A QUESTION OF FACE

I first met Choo Ker Yong at the Apex Club where we were both members in the 1970s. Apex Club comprises young people who wish to do charity work and is like a younger version of the Rotary Club. Both of us belonged to Apex Club East, Singapore. We were affiliated to the worldwide Apex movement with its headquarters in Australia.

We became friends and every time after a Club dinner, we would go out for drinks. One day, he asked me which area of law practice I was in. At that time I said I was doing general work and would take on anything that came along as I was starting out in my career and couldn't afford to be choosy as a young lawyer. He laughed and said, "I have a case from my company that I would like you to handle."

Choo Ker Yong is a director of Cheng Meng Furniture Group (Pte) Ltd. As far as I know, the company does very good interior renovation work for many five-star hotels. So, naturally, I thought that he had a monetary claim against a client who had not settled after work had been done, but he said that it was a landlord and tenant matter. His company was the principal tenant and they had been collecting money from the sub-tenants all those years. However, one particular sub-tenant had suddenly refused to pay to them, saying that he would only pay to the landlord directly. The sub-tenant did not recognise my client as the principal tenant. I said, "Oh, it sounds simple enough.

I will ask him to pay the rent directly to your company." He replied, "Ya, it sounds simple. So can I send someone over to your office with the documents?"

The next day I received the documents. We sent a letter of demand to the sub-tenant who had stubbornly refused to pay the rent to them. They replied through a lawyer called David Chelliah, who used to be a Senior Partner of Drew & Napier, in a letter that was quite arrogant. So I decided to apply for an order for summary judgement. A summary judgement is a judgement that you try to obtain without a trial, stating to the court that the facts of law are so obvious that the defendant has no defence. I filed the affidavit of Choo Ker Yong's father, stating the facts as to why he is the principal tenant and why the other side should pay to him.

The response to that affidavit came immediately. It was about 74 pages long, stating the law and facts. Here was a man who's not educated in law, stating the facts of law. To me this was strange and the matter was getting more intense. Before I could complete reading the defendant's affidavit, a second affidavit was served. This second affidavit was approximately 90 pages long, stating practically everything that was in the first affidavit with some additional facts. I was getting flustered and worried.

While looking at the file, I thought, "What have I got myself into? This seems to be very complicated." While I was contemplating the situation, my secretary approached me and said, "There is a Mr Choo Cheng Meng who wants to see you without an appointment." I told her, "Oh my goodness, this is the man himself, the boss of Cheng Meng Furniture."

I walked over to the reception, greeted him with a handshake and said, "Mr Choo, what can I do for you?" He said, "You can do a lot for me, dear young man. You are my son's good friend. He wanted me to give this case to you. I don't know who you are and I feel you are too young and inexperienced in such matters. We wanted to instruct our company's solicitors but Ker Yong insisted that we should try out other people, especially young upstarts. This is the reason why I agreed to instruct you." He asked, "How is the matter coming along?" I assured him that it was going on well.

Mr Choo said to me, "Mr Anandan, I do not want any excuses. I do not want to lose this case because now it is a matter of face. My whole clan is watching to see what is going to happen. If this person doesn't pay the rent to me, the remaining sub-tenants will also not pay to me. I don't mind them paying directly to the landlord because whatever I collect from them I give to the landlord but I want to be recognised as the principal tenant. At least he should make one payment directly to me after which I will make arrangements for him to pay to the landlord. So there is no question of losing. We must win." I said, "I will do my best." He replied, "Your best is not good enough. I want you to tell me that you will win."

Of course it was difficult for me to assure him that we would win the case and I reiterated to him, "It is difficult for me to say that I will win but I will do my best." With that response, he said to me, "I was told that there are very smart lawyers in England. If necessary, you ask them for help. If not, you can fly to London with my son to consult one of them. I am prepared to give you the money because I don't want to lose. Is that understood?" I agreed with him. He emphasised, "Money is no issue but my face is very important to me. So you make sure you win the case for me, OK?" He stood up, shook my hand with his big strong hand, reminding me that he was once a great carpenter. Today he is the Chairman of one of the biggest furniture companies in

Singapore. You look at the man and you can see his determination but I could also see his warmth and kindness.

After he left, I sat down and tried to contact Ker Yong who was overseas. I told myself that I couldn't afford to lose this case. Although Mr Choo had instructed me to engage a Queen's Counsel, I felt that I did not need to do so. Then it struck me, "Ah, Chan Sek Keong, my Pupil Master!" I did my six months' pupilage training under him. I thought, "I shall seek his advice. He will be able to assist me. He will definitely be able to handle this matter."

I called his secretary and told her that I would like to brief Sek Keong on this matter. I emphasised the urgency and wanted to meet with him as soon as possible. This was in the afternoon and later that afternoon, she called back to inform me that Sek Keong would see me in the morning the next day. I agreed. She said to me, "Don't be late!" I assured her that I would be punctual as I take my practice seriously unlike the days when I was a pupil with Chan Sek Kong. She laughed.

At 11 o'clock the next morning, I took the whole file with all the relevant documents to Shook Lin & Bok. I met with Sek Keong and he enquired, "What is the problem?" I handed the file to him and upon seeing the affidavits, he smiled and asked me, "You got frightened by these affidavits?" My reply was, "I'm not frightened but I got confused and worried." I shared with him what Choo Cheng Meng had said to me. I said I needed him to be the lead counsel and I would be the instructing solicitor. As expected, he assured me, "No problem, we shall do that." He took over the matter and a date was fixed for an Order 14 application to be heard. Chan Sek Keong and I represented the plaintiffs and David Chelliah and his assistant for the defendant. We all appeared before the Registrar, Roderick Martin, to argue the case for summary judgement.

After listening to the arguments and counter arguments from both sides, Rodrick Martin ordered a summary judgement. He then told David Chelliah that he was actually wasting his time putting up a sham defence. Our clients had been quite reasonable and the defendant only needed to make one payment to them and they would have made arrangements for the defendant to deal directly with the landlord. He also noted that the defendant was being stubborn. David Chelliah stated that it was a matter of face and I replied that it was certainly a matter of face for everyone. Anyway, I left the court with Chan Sek Keong feeling very happy that we had won. Immediately, I rang Ker Yong to tell him the good news that the judgement was in our favour. His father came on the line and said, "I am very glad you have won the case for me."

Before we could really rejoice in our victory, David Chelliah filed a Notice of Appeal against the decision. Our happiness was short-lived. We did not know what the Appellate Judge would do regarding the decision of Roderick Martin. We found out later that the Judge who would be hearing the case was Justice AP Rajah. He would sit as vacation judge because this case was being heard during vacation. Once again we trooped into Justice AP Rajah's Chambers for arguments. Strangely, he could only recognise David Chelliah and me. I had to introduce Chan Sek Keong to him. If AP Rajah were alive, I don't think he could ever imagine that Chan Sek Keong would one day be the Chief Justice of Singapore.

The arguments commenced and it went on for the whole morning. AP Rajah dismissed the appeal of David Chelliah and said, "Actually, Mr Chelliah, there is no merit to this appeal at all. I do not know why you bothered to appeal. You make me work during vacation for this. I am ordering costs at the higher scale."

There were scales of costs then. It was the discretion of the Judge to order the cost and in this case, he ordered the highest scale of costs. We thanked him and as we walked out of court, Sek Keong asked David Chelliah, "Are you going to the Court of Appeal? You are bound to lose again. I am not being arrogant but it is quite clear that you will lose again. So why don't you discuss this with your client and we will make sure that he pays the money to our clients who will hand the money to the landlord. We will ask the landlord to give everybody who is the sub-tenant of our clients, separate leases so that they can all deal directly with the landlord." Our clients were quite happy to relinquish their responsibilities as the principal tenants.

Two days later we received a reply from David Chelliah stating that his client was prepared to pay the rent to our clients and in return, our clients would negotiate for a new lease for him with the landlord. We managed to obtain a new lease for him and for all the other sub-tenants as well.

A happy Choo Cheng Meng asked his son, Ker Yong, to take me out for dinner and to ask me to bill for work done. It was not important to settle my fee for work done but it was definitely a must to settle Chan Sek Keong's bill as he did most part of the work in his office. He also learnt that Sek Keong loved to collect antique wood and they settled the matter with him very amicably.

The reason I include this case is to show how people react and act at times. There was no need for the sub-tenant to go to court. There was no need for Cheng Meng Furniture to take them to court; but because it was a question of 'face' they were prepared to spend thousands of dollars in costs to prove a point and save their faces. Sometimes I think to myself, "Lawyers can never go hungry in Singapore as long as there are stubborn and proud people, where parties do not exhibit common sense and understanding, and where they just want to prove a point." I went on to act for Cheng Meng Furniture on many other matters and I became a friend of Choo Cheng Meng. I still see him sometimes at the same restaurant, being helped by his daughter. Each time we meet, he would say that we must have lunch together some day. I, too, would say the same to him. I mentioned to Ker Yong who visits me often that I need to have lunch with his ageing father and he assured me that he would arrange it. I insisted that it should be soon as we were both ailing in health, so let it not be a disappointment if something should happen to one of us. He assured me that both his father and I would live long but he would still arrange lunch as soon as he could.

There was another case where I had to brief Chan Sek Keong again. This was a family dispute involving millions of dollars. I found that it was something I should not handle because I was not experienced or knowledgeable enough to do the case. Sek Keong did it and we succeeded again. Our clients managed to get what they wanted. I thought at the time that Sek Keong was one of the best lawyers you could come across and I knew that he was fated for bigger things but I never thought that he would become the Attorney-General and then the Chief Justice of Singapore.

After his appointment as Chief Justice, I was one of three criminal lawyers he called upon to assess our opinion on the present criminal legal system. I was very candid. I told him which Subordinate Courts judges should be transferred out to somewhere remote so that they could not do harm. The other two lawyers were shocked at my blunt accusations against these judges but Sek Keong laughed and said, "This is something I expect from Subhas. He doesn't mince his words." The two lawyers laughed.

TWENTY-THREE

CLASH WITH THE LAW SOCIETY

Ten years ago, in 2004, together with a few other lawyers, we formed the Association of Criminal Lawyers, Singapore (ACLS), an organisation set up to look after the interests of criminal lawyers. We did this as we felt that the Law Society was not doing enough. We started with around 100 members and I was elected the first President of the Association.

When Chan Sek Keong became the Chief Justice of Singapore, he asked Bala Reddy, who was the first Community Court Judge, to see if he could get the ACLS to send volunteers to help those who were not represented by lawyers. Bala Reddy, who is an old friend, called me to convey the Chief Justice's request. He asked, "Would you help?" I replied, "Sure, we would like to help especially in the Community Courts where they deal with teenage delinquents and mentally challenged individuals." In a matter of time, ACLS was doing a better job than the Law Society's Criminal Legal Aid Scheme (CLAS) which also provided free services.

The Law Society President at the time was Wong Meng Meng. I did not like his arrogance but I admire him for being a brilliant lawyer and for his unwavering principles although I do not agree with them. He stood by his principles and defended them however much you criticised him; and in that sense, I like his courage.

Once, an Extra-Ordinary General Meeting was held to pass a 'No Confidence Vote' against him and the Council of the Law Society. This clash came about because during a trial session in the High Court, a member of the Law Society had produced a letter from the psychiatrist of M Ravi, another lawyer, casting doubts on his ability to practise because of a relapse of his bipolar disorder. No action was taken against the member for his unethical conduct. We wanted Wong Meng Meng to be removed as President. He said that he didn't have to step down. He would show by his conduct that he was not biased. While the arguments were going on, many of us spoke for his removal. At the same time, there were others who spoke in support of him.

The clash between Wong Meng Meng and me led to dire consequences. The newspapers got out of hand, publishing all sorts of stories. One day at a function, Chief Justice Chan Sek Keong saw me and said, "You know, Subhas, I don't care who is wrong or who is right. This war in the newspapers must stop." When I tried to explain to him, he said, "No, please, I am not interested in any explanation. There shouldn't be anymore bad references that allow the public to have a bad image of the legal fraternity." He walked away after saying that.

I looked at him and thought, "Here is the Chief Justice who seems to be more interested in keeping the newspapers away than finding out what is the root cause of the problem between me and the Law Society President who happens to be his good friend." It seemed as though transparency did not exist here.

The Chief Justice was not the same person I knew when I was his pupil. Furthermore, he was also not in favour of the ACLS taking a permanent role in some aspects of criminal law. It was decided at one time that there would be four lunches per year, each one hosted by the Law Society, ACLS, the Judiciary and the Attorney-General's Chambers

(AGC). However, at the first lunch, the Chief Justice mentioned in his speech that there would only be three lunches, and they were to be hosted by the Law Society, the Judiciary and the AGC.

ACLS was quietly kicked out. He didn't want to give us any importance

At an ACLS lunch, September 2011. From left: Justice Choo Han Teck, Chief Justice Chan Sek Keong and Subhas.

but it didn't matter to us as our main focus and commitment was pro bono work and we saved money by not hosting a lunch. However, we were not happy with his attitude. We never tried to compete with any other associations and ACLS did its best to supplement the actions of the Law Society. There was a healthy relationship between the two associations until Wong Meng Meng became President of the Law Society.

Anyway, sadly and with some regret, my clashes with Wong Meng Meng created inconvenience to quite a lot of people because in his personal life he was well-liked with a section of lawyers and so was I. He stood down after his term was over and passed on the baton to his vice-president, Loke Vi Meng.

In my opinion, the Law Society has become a defunct and lost organisation. When I was first called to the Bar in 1971, it was a prestigious organisation comprising Council Members who were illustrious people. It was a small Secretariat and the then President ran it well. He managed with what he had. Now the membership of the Law Society has flourished and it has become an organisation run by many employed directors.

It is one of those bad days for me during dialysis. I just feel depressed because I've been told that there may be a blockage in my vein and I may need to go for ballooning. The consequences may not be that good. I seem to get bad news all the time and I don't know why. I am being punished for my sins. I think the punishment is exceeding whatever sins I may have committed in my life. I have come to the conclusion that God is not really fair. He is, after all, just a God. I feel sometimes that He doesn't have the ability and strength that I thought He had in righting all wrongs in this world.

TWENTY-FOUR

CHIEF JUSTICES

I have had the privilege of practising during the terms of four Chief Justices. They are Wee Chong Jin, the first Chief Justice (CJ) when I was called to the Bar in January 1971, Yong Pung How, Chan Sek Keong and currently, Sundaresh Menon.

Let me share with you certain perceptions of these four Chief Justices. They might not like what I have to say but then I have always said what I have felt like saying if I believe it is true.

WEE CHONG JIN (1963 – 1990)

Wee Chong Jin, the first Chief Justice, was a very intelligent person and his knowledge of the law was second to none. His judgements were simple to understand but a Chief Justice's job is not just writing judgements. He has to be a good administrator, too. In my opinion, CJ Wee Chong Jin was not a good administrator. Some said he tried but when the demands that he made from the authorities for better pay and better people were not met, it seems he became frustrated. He left the administration of the courts to various registrars and the staff and did not bother to look into it. Most of his time was spent playing golf. I believe he loved golf more than law, so much so that there was a backlog of cases as far back as five to six years. Parties had to wait that long before they could hear their civil cases. It was worse for criminal cases as the accused persons had to stay in remand prison for as long as between five and seven years for their trial to be heard, and if they were acquitted for the offence, no compensation was paid for their time in prison. Such was the situation in the system that made many angry. The perception was that the he didn't seem to bother. In the end, when he was to retire, many said that it was high time that he left and a more efficient system be put in place.

My encounters with Wee Chong Jin were quite funny. In the beginning when I appeared before him, I had good hearings as I was always prepared and he would grant me whatever I wanted. This made Glenn Knight, who was Deputy Public Prosecutor, comment one day, "With the Chief Justice, we have no chance. Whatever this guy asks for, he gets it."

However, subsequently, when I was acting for JB Jeyaretnam (JBJ), his whole attitude towards me changed. He was extremely rude to me, extremely unreasonable and for the smallest of faults, he would rebuke me as though I had committed a capital offence. I took it all because as far as I was concerned, I was not going to let the attitude of anybody stop me from doing the best for my client. Subsequently, we won the JBJ case in the Privy Council. The Chief Justice, judges and others involved in the administration of justice were admonished by the Privy Council which had very harsh words to say about some of our High Court Judges. That made matters even worse but the Chief Justice was going to retire.

Before he retired though, Wee Chong Jin wanted to start the Academy of Law and he told the Registrar of the Supreme Court to inform me that he wanted me to be in one of the sub-committees. Together with the then Law Society President, Giam Chin Toon, he invited me for lunch at the Academy of Law Restaurant. He made it quite clear that he was leaving soon and wanted to leave without any misunderstandings between us. He was extremely friendly to me and told me to work hard as this public relations sub-committee was very important. He knew that I was the right person to be in the committee. It was quite a strange coincidence that after the lunch, as the three of us were walking out of the restaurant, we came face to face with JBJ. He looked surprised when he saw me. As soon as I reached my office, I received a phone call from him asking, "What's happening? Are you changing sides?" I replied, "There is no question of me changing sides, Ben, as I was not on anybody's side. I was invited for lunch and I went. That was all."

At the opening of the Academy of Law, Mr Lee Kuan Yew, then Prime Minister of Singapore, was invited. He was mingling with the lawyers and his security noticed that I was in the area that was restricted only to organisers and committee members. His surprised bodyguards asked Lawrence Quahe, then an Assistant Registrar of the Supreme Court, "Isn't he Subhas?" Lawrence jokingly replied, "Yes, he is but not to worry. Today he's on our side." With that, everyone laughed.

YONG PUNG HOW (1990 – 2006)

When Yong Pung How was brought in as a High Court Judge for one year under CJ Wee Chong Jin, we all knew that he would be the next Chief Justice. It was quite clear that he was appointed for a particular purpose. We were also aware that one of the judges who would be disappointed with this appointment would be Justice Lai Kew Chai because he had been tipped to be the next Chief Justice.

There was no doubt CJ Yong Pung How was a very efficient administrator. He revamped the administrative structure of the judiciary and made sure that the backlog of cases was dealt with efficiently and expeditiously. All new cases that were coming up for hearing had a deadline. He also ensured that all cases, from the time of the arrest of an accused person to the time of his trial and conviction or acquittal, would be heard within a span of six months to a year and an appeal thereafter within six months. A far cry from when Wee Chong Jin was the Chief Justice. Singapore suddenly had one of the most efficient legal systems in the world. One could say that the new system worked like clock work.

However, the problem with Yong Pung How was his attitude towards the accused person and counsel. His statements from the Bench could be hurting and sarcastic. He gave the impression that all accused persons who stood before him were guilty; otherwise they wouldn't be there in the first place. He said many times from the Bench, "The Police don't simply charge anyone for no reason. The DPP doesn't come to court to prosecute for nothing. There must be some strong evidence against the accused person." Counsels who appeared before him were treated very shoddily, especially criminal lawyers.

However, I got along quite well with him and I had a fair amount of success before him. Others would ask me, "How does that happen?" I said, "When you are arguing and he shows disinterest in one of the points, go on to the next point. Don't waste his time. He appreciates that and if he is interested in the next point you are arguing, he will give it more credit because you have not wasted his time. He expects you to be brief, to the point and don't try to persuade him by using the wrong tactics."

One of the cases where I appeared before CJ Yong Pung How was the one that Melanie Ho took over from Edmond Pereira. She wanted me to argue it while we were colleagues in Harry Elias Partnership. The accused, who was the chief of police at the airport, had been convicted and sent to jail for charges under the Police Act. We were briefed to quash the conviction but more importantly to ensure that he didn't have to go to jail. Just before my turn came to argue, the counsel for the earlier appeal made Yong Pung How angry. The CJ said to him, "I don't care what your client or your client's family think, but let it be known that I am a hard-hearted Justice who stands for no nonsense. I have no compassion for this sort of cases." He dismissed the appeal.

So when it was my turn, I started arguing on the conviction part. The Chief Justice quite clearly told me that he was not with me on this argument and insisted that I should move on to the next point. I said, "If your Honour is not with me on the appeal on the conviction, then may I start with my appeal against sentence." He allowed me to go ahead. I continued, "Your Honour, I heard what you said to the other counsel about you being a hard-nosed hard-hearted Judge with no compassion. I think you definitely said it out of anger because…" As I tried to explain further, he retorted, "Of course, I have compassion. You should know since I have heard so many of your clients' appeals." I replied, "That was what I wanted to say. You have shown compassion to my other clients. I hope that you will look at this case in a very sympathetic manner." I put forward my case. He then told me, "I don't think this man deserves to go to jail. I will convert it to a fine." He gave a fine for each of the offences for which my client was sentenced — that was two offences at $500 each. My client and I left the court feeling very happy. He said to me, "You were flattering the Judge just now." I denied it and explained, "I was just stating a fact. Anyway, it doesn't matter even if I was praising him or not, he allowed the appeal."

You see, Chief Justice Yong Pung How had his own unique way of thinking. There were certain cases where he was adamant about not allowing the appeal. I have noticed that he was least sympathetic towards sexual offenders. In another case where I appeared before him, I told him that the Judge had called for both probation and reformative training. Both were recommended but he decided to send my client to the Reformative Training Centre. I felt it was not fair. I argued and tried to persuade the Chief Justice by pleading my case as to why probation was necessary. After listening to me, he said, "Mr Anandan, I came this morning to dismiss your appeal and to scold you for this appeal, but you have persuaded me otherwise. I am allowing probation. You are one of those quick-witted Advocates who have appeared before me." I thanked him and walked out of court.

When I got back to the office, our Senior Partner, Harry Elias, was there. He was pleased to see me and said, "Hey, I heard what the Chief Justice said about you. It's high time for you to apply for Senior Counsel." I replied, "Ah, it really doesn't matter."

This brings to mind a day in December 1987 when, along with Vimi and a few other lawyers and their spouses, I was invited to the Istana to have lunch with President Wee Kim Wee and Mrs Wee. I was assigned a seat beside President Wee. He asked me, "Is it true that in Singapore you have to prove that you are innocent and until then you are deemed to be guilty?" I looked at him and thought, "Is this man serious or is he joking?" I then realised that he was completely serious about the question. I assured him, "No, Mr President. The presumption of innocence is still there but somehow because of certain judgements and certain pronouncements by members of the Bench, the public seems to think that the burden has shifted." With eyes wide, he replied, "Wow, I am very happy that they are still presumed innocent till they are proven guilty."

CHAN SEK KEONG (2006 – 2012)

The third appointed Chief Justice was Chan Sek Keong. He was first appointed Attorney-General in 1992. He held that appointment till 2006 when he took over as CJ from CJ Yong Pung How.

In addition to what I have shared in the earlier chapters, my opinion of Chan Sek Keong is that out of all the Chief Justices, he was the most well informed. He was an intellectual, well read and very knowledgeable in many aspects of the law. He was an external examiner in the National University of Singapore and his reputation as a Jurist was known far and wide. He was respected abroad and did well in arguing Singapore's case against Malaysia in the dispute of the Pedra Branca Island.

He was very capable and his experience as Attorney-General and later on the Bench as a High Court Judge made him an all-rounder. He was exceptionally good in his law and was equipped with the right judicial temperament. So when he left, we were quite upset as we thought that we were losing a very capable and moderate Chief Justice.

However, he did little to improve the judicial system and only maintained it as it was, simply because of the efficiency of his predecessor. He just continued with the same system and fine-tuned the judgements of the High Court Judges. Suddenly, lawyers found that the Magistrate's Court Appeals, which were once deemed a frightening experience, were becoming better in the sense that lawyers were given full hearings without interruption and without sarcastic remarks. We found that the Appellate Court Judges were serious in their consideration of the Appeals and most of them wrote good judgements although some judges wrote judgements that were too short. Notable judgements were from the present Attorney-General, VK Rajah, who was then Justice of Appeal. His judgements showed compassion and wisdom. Appellate Court decisions were becoming more respected because of the quality of the judgements.

SUNDARESH MENON (current, since 2012)

Members of the Bar thought that VK Rajah, Justice of Appeal, would succeed CJ Chan Sek Keong as the new Chief Justice but it was not to be. In 2012, CJ Chan Sek Keong was succeeded by Sundaresh Menon, who was the Attorney-General and was later appointed Justice of Appeal for a few months before becoming Chief Justice.

The moment Sundaresh Menon was transferred to the Judiciary from his position as the Attorney-General, we all knew that he would be the next Chief Justice because the writing on the wall was quite clear.

I thought that VK Rajah would be the automatic choice for the position as he had all the qualities and he was very popular with the Bar because of his fair decisions. So it naturally came as a surprise when he was bypassed. I actually felt quite unhappy that he was bypassed, but then in our system there are situations that cannot be explained, situations that you had better not try to explain as it could lead you into trouble.

Chief Justice Sundaresh Menon continued the work of CJ Chan Sek Keong. He brought in a lot of changes and while, up till now, we still have not seen exactly what improvements he will be providing, one thing is certain: he gave the Subordinate Court Judges a sense of importance. He changed the name to The State Courts of Singapore. He also made the judges wear robes, I think with the hope that they will take their responsibilities very seriously.

An editorial in the ACLS magazine, *Pro Bono*, questioned why the Subordinate Court Judges had to wear robes, when everywhere else the robes were being taken off. Furthermore the stature of the man did not depend on his robes but the quality of the judgement he gave. Before the magazine was circulated, it was sent to Chief District Judge Tan Siong Thye for his comments. All hell broke loose with Jennifer Marie, the Deputy Chief District Judge. She called me and insisted that I should go to the Subordinate Courts that evening at 5:00 pm. I wanted to know what all the urgency was about and she replied, "Don't tell me you don't know?" I replied, "Yes, I don't." She explained further, "Your editorial in the *Pro Bono*. We need to discuss it." At that point, I honestly was not aware of what she was referring to but I didn't want to let her know that too.

I called up some of the ACLS committee members and we went to see Tan Siong Thye. He was a little flustered and asked me, "What is this all about?" He said CJ Sundaresh Menon was very angry with me. By then I had learnt that it was about the editorial and I defended it. I said, "What is wrong with the contents of the article? We are entitled to speak our mind." He replied, "The Chief Justice wants to know what we have to say on this and to speak to you about it." I explained that we had nothing more to add and were entitled to comment if there was any change, even if it was a change in the dress code of the Bench. We were afraid that soon the Bar would be required to wear robes in the Subordinate Courts too.

The arguments continued and I told him that I would think about it. I went back and discussed the matter with the ACLS committee. I told them, "We have been trying to build up a good rapport between the Judiciary and the Bar and this article is not going to help." We decided that we would stop circulating that particular edition.

CJ Sundaresh Menon's anger was obvious when he practically ignored me at a function, but it didn't bother me. Sometimes you please some people, sometimes you don't. I think he did not know that I had already decided not to circulate that edition. At another function I happened to be at the same table as the Chief Justice. (By then, I had told the Chief Justice that I had ordered for that edition of the magazine to be withdrawn.) He tapped me on the shoulder and said, "You know, Subhas, we worked very hard on our Bench and Bar relationship with so many committees and that article would have set us back a few steps." I agreed and said, "That's exactly why I decided not to circulate it." He laughed and said, "Very wise decision."

A few days after that, I had lunch with K. Shanmugam, the Minister for Law. He asked me, "Why are you giving the Chief Justice a headache?" I denied it and explained the situation to him. The Honourable Minister laughed and said, "There must be some excitement sometimes."

So I realised one thing. For Chief Justice Sundaresh Menon, the rapport between the Judiciary and the Bar is more important than whether it is fair to comment or whether you have the right to comment. What means more to him is that everyone works well together to make the system more effective. I certainly do not have any complaints about that.

On the whole, my experiences with CJ Sundaresh Menon have been good. When he was Attorney-General, I had lunches with him to discuss certain aspects of the law that had to be changed. He was a very reasonable man, very intelligent and quick to grasp whatever you are saying. When he was appointed the Chief Justice, I wrote a congratulatory letter to him to which he graciously replied.

TWENTY-FIVE

ATTORNEY-GENERALS

I have also had the privilege of practising during the appointments of several Attorney-Generals (AG). Here are my recollections of some of them.

TAN BOON TEIK (1969 – 1992)

Tan Boon Teik was the first Attorney-General of Singapore when I first started practice in January 1971. He was the longest serving AG, holding the office first as Acting Attorney-General from 1967 to 1968 and then as Attorney-General from 1969 to 1992. Members of the Criminal Bar were not particularly fond of him but for some reason, he was maintained in office for a long time.

There was nothing outstanding about the man and there are many situations that I could comment on him. However, the man is gone and I wish to let it be but I must mention that he tried to complain against me to the Law Society. He said that I should be struck off for misconduct when I handled JB Jeyaretnam's case.

The Inquiry Committee found that some of the allegations needed to go before the Disciplinary Committee, which was then chaired by the retired Supreme Court Judge Choor Singh. I was represented earlier on by Chong Yuen Hee, a very senior lawyer. Subsequently, I appointed Francis Seow, the ex-Solicitor-General and the then-to-be President of the Law Society. I must also point out that when Francis Seow was the Solicitor-General, he could not see eye to eye with Tan Boon Teik.

When we appeared before the Disciplinary Committee, the Law Society was represented by H.P. Godwin, another senior lawyer, and assisted by a young lawyer. They told the Chairman, Choor Singh, that the Law Society was not adducing any evidence against me. They had taken an opinion from the highest authorities and had decided that they would not adduce against me. Choor Singh was surprised and said, "Maybe he has not done anything particular under this section of the Legal Profession Act but look at the other sections. Have you looked at them?" Dumbfounded, Godwin said, "We have looked at all the various sections and as far as we are concerned, Mr Anandan has committed no offence. He cannot be charged for misconduct under any section of the Legal Profession Act. This is the stand of the Law Society."

Of course, Choor Singh was very disappointed because he was looking forward to hearing the case. The other person who was also disappointed was my own defence counsel, Francis Seow. He was looking forward to cross-examining the AG Tan Boon Teik.

Anyway, Choor Singh wrote to Chief Justice Wee Chong Jin and as far as the Law Society was concerned, it was the end of the matter. Of course if Tan Boon Teik wanted to appeal, he could have done it in his own personal capacity. In that case, if he were to lose, he would have to pay costs. He decided not to appeal. Many said that that was the finest moment of the Law Society. It was the first time the Law Society had decided that they would not adduce evidence against their own member. However, the Law Society then and the Law Society now are totally different. The members of the Law Society Council then were made of sterner stuff than those who came on later.

After Tan Boon Teik retired from office, Chan Sek Keong became the Attorney-General in 1992. He was a High Court Judge before he was transferred to the Attorney-General's Chambers.

WALTER WOON (2008 – 2010)

Walter Woon was first an academic and then a diplomat and a politician. He was appointed the Second Solicitor-General under the then Attorney-General Chao Hick Tin in 2006. The following year, he was appointed Solicitor-General, and then became Attorney-General from 2008 to 2010. He is well known as an academic and has written books on Company Law. He was also an ambassador of Singapore. As a Nominated Member of Parliament, he was the first Member of Parliament since 1965 to have a Private Member's Bill become a public law in Singapore. That was the Maintenance of Parents Act which was passed in 1995.

Walter Woon was held in high regard by both the Bar and the academics. We in the Criminal Bar expected many positive changes from Professor Woon. In some ways, we were disappointed because we felt that he was very hard on accused persons. As the AG, he didn't have the same compassion as others had. Personally, I think it was his lack of exposure to practice and, being an academic first, he was a man who would command by the book.

There was the case of Aniza Bte Essa where this woman used her lover, a 16-year-old boy, to kill her husband. The teenager was my client and he was given detention at the President's pleasure. As the woman was suffering from a mental ailment, her charge was reduced to culpable homicide. The Trial Judge sentenced her to nine years in prison when he could have given her ten years or life. The prosecution decided to appeal and I was surprised that the Attorney-General himself came to argue the Appeal and to tell the Court of Appeal why they should give this woman a life sentence. I was familiar with this case because Noor Mohd Marican, the lawyer for Aniza, was consulting me in many aspects and I was in court during the hearing to observe.

Walter Woon greeted me and we were cordial to one another. In my mind I was thinking that there was no way he was going to succeed in this appeal because the courts are not prepared to make drastic decisions on accused persons who were unwell.

This woman had been certified mentally ill. So how could he ask for life imprisonment? He did, and from the word "go" he was getting a tough time because the Judges were interrupting him and asking him questions. The way they reacted to his answers showed that they were not impressed. Subsequently, they asked Noor Marican to reply. Marican, in his own way, said what he had to say, that the Learned Trial Judge who had sentenced his client to nine years was absolutely right and there was no reason for the Court of Appeal to change it. Eventually, the Court of Appeal did not interfere. They did not even raise the sentence an extra year, to ten years. This was to show that what the Attorney-General was asking for could not be allowed because of the sympathy they had for the accused person who was mentally ill.

By arguing this appeal personally, Walter Woon's reputation was tarnished. The Bar said that he was ruthless and some of my clients wondered why this case was so important that he had to prosecute the matter himself. There was no clarification.

It was during his term as Attorney-General that I wrote an article stating that there was a law for the rich and another law for the poor. When it came to composition of offences, I cited several cases that showed that there were stark discrepancies of compounding offences between the rich and the poor. There was a huge uproar and the Law

Ministry replied saying that I was absolutely wrong and explained that it was not the situation. I remember replying when I was hospitalised in December 2008, stating that I stand by what I said as I have statistics to prove my case.

During that time, we had invited Walter Woon to give a lecture at the Association of Criminal Lawyers of Singapore's (ACLS) annual lecture and he had accepted. When I received him at the entrance of the Supreme Court, he said, "Am I expected to reply to your article during this lecture?" I assured him that he could and he should. He added, "Did you write that article to create controversy?" I replied, "No. I wrote it because I felt that it had to be written and at the time I was writing, it was because of a particular case." He said, "I do not want to comment about it right now but I will touch on it in my lecture, if you don't mind." Of course, I didn't mind.

During the lecture, he referred to my article and said that there were reasons why sometimes composition of offences could not be allowed. There could not be any transparency because of particular security reasons; for reasons that they had to review police investigation; and that was the reason there seemed to be this perception that the rich found it easier to compound offences.

When my turn came to wind up the lecture, after the question and answer session, I told the audience that I felt that I got away "cheaply". Everybody laughed.

Walter Woon's tenure as AG was for two years. It ended in April 2010 and was not renewed. After the two years, he went back to lecture in the university and, clearly, back to the academic world. Walter Woon is a very good lecturer and the students who have been taught by him have a very high regard for him. So I think it turned out well that he went back to academia.

SUNDARESH MENON (2010 – 2012)

Koh Juat Jong stood in as Acting Attorney-General for an interim period from April to October 2010, after which Sundaresh Menon was appointed the new Attorney-General. He held office for two years from 2010 to 2012. He is now the Chief Justice.

We realised that Sundaresh Menon was very relaxed with the practising members of the Bar simply because he was a practising lawyer before his appointment as Attorney-General. He found it very easy to deal with our problems because he had seen them himself when he was a lawyer. However, after a two-year tenure as AG, he was appointed as the Justice of Appeal of the Supreme Court and we wondered why. As the Attorney-General, he had been very effective and we appreciated the way he dealt with issues. Some people felt then that he was posted to the Supreme Court possibly because he would be the next Chief Justice.

STEVEN CHONG (2012 – 2014)

Steven Chong was appointed Attorney-General for the next two years from June 2012 to June 2014.

During his tenure, several public figures and government servants were charged. One of them was acquitted and the other found guilty. We always wondered why the AG decided to charge these people in open court when a disciplinary action would have sufficed and they could have avoided the publicity and mud slinging in Court. Again there were public murmurs as to why a law professor was charged for corruption and for taking gratification from his student. Most people felt that the best thing to do was just to sack the lecturer and at worst, get him out of Singapore. But he was charged. Halfway through trial he defended himself and was convicted. He was serving his sentence while he continued to appeal and the Appellate Court decided that his conviction was wrong.

All these matters did not reflect very well on Steven Chong as Attorney-General. He is a fine lawyer and a very good judge but I think he made some poor judgement calls as AG.

When he came in as Attorney-General, you could see he was different. He wanted to meet the Criminal Bar to seek their co-operation and to get them involved in the Criminal Law system. He met up with the Criminal Bar over a luncheon. He was very approachable and I, as the President of the ACLS, could just call him personally and tell him the problem we had at hand and he would invite me over to have coffee with him to discuss the matter.

However, after two years as Attorney-General, he returned to the High Court Bench and became a Supreme Court Judge. Quite a number of people were happy that he was leaving the Attorney-General's Chambers because they felt that he was better as a judge than as an AG. I have appeared before Steven Chong when he was a judge and I must say that he was a good and fair Judge. He has made a mark for himself dealing with criminal and civil matters.

VK RAJAH (current, since 2014)

After Steven Chong, we were surprised at the announcement that Justice of Appeal, VK Rajah, would be appointed the new Attorney-General. We thought that he would retire from the Bench.

It was a surprise as we could not imagine the Judiciary without VK Rajah because during the time he was there as a judge, he earned the respect of the Criminal and Civil Bar. His judgements were enlightening. His conduct of cases when we appeared before him was fair. He was very courteous but he could be tough when he needed to be. He had all the qualities of a good judge.

So we were not very happy to see him leave the Bench to be the latest Attorney-General in June 2014. However, I have shared with DPPs my pleasure in knowing that he would be bringing along with him all the fine qualities of a good judge to the Attorney-General's Chambers. In this respect, we will have an excellent Attorney-General because one of the main criteria of a good Attorney-General is to be able to exercise discretion judicially and fairly.

I believe that VK Rajah can do it. He has always been a fair person. I accepted, as a friend, his invitation to have *thosai* (Indian crepe) with him one morning and I am looking forward to fixing a date with him. I met him at this year's Hari Raya lunch organised by the Muslim Lawyers Association. I was enjoying the *briyani* as though it was the end of the world when I noticed that he was eating like a bird. He said that he normally eats very little especially during lunch.

Softly he said to me, "You know, Mr Anandan, I can tell you this now since I am not a Judge anymore. The Judiciary has a lot of respect for you because you come straight to the point when you argue your cases without massaging the facts. This earned our respect." I was pleased to hear that and said that it was good to know.

I told him, "Let me share with you something which I could not do so when you were a Judge. You know, when I was in the Socialist Club in the University, I used to visit your father, Mr TT Rajah, because he was our mentor in many ways and we consulted him on issues that we could not understand. Mr TT Rajah was very passionate about what he believed in and being a Socialist, he practised what he preached. He was not materialistic. He was a humble, forthright man with strong conviction in what he believes. It was really a wonderful experience chatting with him. I remember the first time I met him. He looked at me and asked, 'Subhas, do you have any dreams?' I replied to him, 'Mr Rajah, if you don't have dreams when you are young, what sort of life are you leading? I can't imagine a life without dreams.' He smiled and said, 'Good but make sure that your dreams are the right dreams.' With that, all those who were there with me laughed. Then he looked at me and asked, 'Are you a Hindu?' I said, 'Yes.' Then he specified, 'Are you a Hindu by choice or by birth?' I looked at him and said, 'Both.' Everybody laughed and he looked at the rest and said, 'You know, this guy, with the answers he gives, he will be a good lawyer.' VK Rajah was pleased to hear me reminiscing about his father.

I had been to see Mr TT Rajah a number of times and I had seen the Attorney-General as a young boy running around in his shorts. When I told this to VK Rajah, he smiled and said, "So you knew my father well." To me, TT Rajah was one of those whom I admired for what he believed in and he made no apologies for what he believed in. Why should he anyway?

While at dialysis, I was told that Justice of Appeal VK Rajah would be the new Attorney-General on 25 June 2014. In my opinion, he is a very good judge. I believe that as Attorney-General, he would surpass his achievement as Justice of Appeal because any man who has compassion for his fellow human being cannot fail. I sent him a note, congratulating him and reminding him that he still owed me lunch. I received a quick reply from him, thanking me for my congratulatory note, telling me that we can always have lunch. "Ask my PA to arrange. We can have breakfast or lunch." He is that sort of man, humble, unpretentious and always caring. I wish we had more judges like him.

TWENTY-SIX

AT THE CASINO

I spent the last weekend of June 2014 at Marina Bay Sands Hotel. My friend, KS Tan, had reserved a suite so I could stay with my wife and son. He said that this would be somewhere for me to relax and not worry about anything. We checked in last Friday. Vimi and Sujesh went first as I had the regular ACLS meeting to chair.

After the meeting, I joined them with my nephew, Sunil, and my legal associate, Diana Ngiam. We also took the opportunity to visit the casino to understand its operational system as we had a case that required us to do so. It was the first time I was going into this casino.

After dinner, all of us went into the casino. As it seemed like quite a long walk from the hotel to the casino, Vimi asked if I would prefer to sit in a wheelchair so that she could push me around. I didn't quite like that as it would attract too much attention. However, it also meant I could cover a longer distance with her and Sujesh. I am getting used to it now with people staring or asking what I'm doing in a wheelchair.

My main intention of visiting the casino was to understand how it worked, the playing and dealing. I needed to know to help me relate better to my client's case. We started to gamble small just for the fun of it. After all, we had paid $100 each. Some of the people who recognised me approached to talk, wishing me well and saying that they hope I would recover fast. I was very touched by these people and I asked them, "Why do you come here? Is it because you have nothing else to do or is it because you think you will win money."

They said that they enjoy visiting the casino because they want to make money. They have lost quite a lot but hope to recover. Feeling a little concerned for them, I replied, "You could lose more, couldn't you?" With a wide grin, one of them said, "Yes." I asked, "Can you afford it?" There was a silence. I didn't want to push the matter.

I moved around the casino and looked at the people. They all seemed so intense and most of the faces looked unhappy. I could be reading them wrongly. They could well be enjoying themselves with a serious look on their faces and didn't mind paying for it. Everybody was concentrating on his own jackpot machine. They had no time to look at anybody else. I was surprised that these people could spend hours gambling, just sitting there and playing the jackpot machines.

I felt I should not need to pay the $100 entrance fee that was compulsory for Singaporeans. Here in my own country, I am being discriminated by the authorities. Menial and casual workers who hold foreign passports are allowed to go in for free while citizens like us are charged $100. What is the rationale behind this requirement, I do not know. It still doesn't deter the frequent hardcore gamblers as they are allowed to walk in any time if they possess an annual pass for just $2,000. In my opinion, it seems to be yet another money making situation by the authorities. Even without an annual pass, $100 is not going to stop a gambler from walking into the casino.

Mr Lee Kuan Yew was adamant that there should be no casinos in Singapore. He was right. However, the younger generation of leaders saw that having a casino in our country could mean a permanent source of generating income. There was little consideration for the ills of society that come with it. Not only one casino was built, but two! They might be making money but at what risks and costs? Having immersed myself in the atmosphere of the casino, I can't help wondering how many people there can actually afford to gamble. So many social ills have come about because of these casinos but nobody seems to care about that. Everybody is interested in making money, including the authorities. There is no other rationale behind having two casinos other than the fact that we are just interested in making money, hopefully from foreigners. But sadly, it has also tempted and victimised several of our citizens.

I realise even more so how casinos contribute to the ills of society when clients walk into my office after committing offences — not only in the casinos but thefts and robbery that they were desperate enough to commit just so they could go to the casinos to gamble again. I wonder whether these casinos are good for the country in the long run or will they destroy our social fabric. I don't think gambling centres like the casinos can be of help or any good to any country. It is immoral for these casinos to exist.

TWENTY-SEVEN

1963: LOYOLA COLLEGE

While sitting here at dialysis and wondering how long more I have to take this, my mind wandered to my growing up years. They were some of the best years of my life. However, I couldn't help but remember the three months I spent in India, in the city of Madras (Chennai).

After my 'O' level exams, where I obtained a First Grade that made my parents very proud, as I wrote in my first book, my mother realised that I would not qualify for pre-medicine 'A' level because I had failed in Chemistry. She wanted me to be a doctor just like Chechy and she was not going to let my failure in Chemistry be a hindrance or obstacle. She decided that she should send me to India where my Chemistry result did not matter; my other grades would suffice. In some ways, I was a very obedient son and tried my best to please my parents. Although I was reluctant to go to India and leave behind all my family and friends, I thought I should give it a try just to please my mother whom I love very dearly.

In March 1963, I left for Madras after a short stint in Bartley Secondary School studying for 'A' Level in the arts stream. I enrolled at Loyola College, the best college in South India and maybe even in the whole of India then. My parents sent me to Madras because my father had a distant relative there. He was Sreedharan and he ran a hotel called Hotel Malabar Hill. His wife, Ravamma, was one of the first people in that era to receive a PhD in Music. They had agreed to be my guardians while I was there. My Chechy was in New Delhi at the time studying for her medical degree and the fact that I had family to look after me gave my parents a greater sense of security.

And so I took my first flight out of Singapore. Although I was excited, I was crying throughout in the plane. The person who sat beside me was also a student but it was not his first flight out of Singapore. He had been travelling in and out of India for more than three years. He put his arm around my shoulders and said, "Is this the first time you are leaving your family? It must be hard but you will get used to it." I cried as I was already missing my family and friends. Holding back my tears, I looked at him with half a smile and said, "I hope that I will feel better as I am feeling very miserable at the moment."

Subhas at the airport leaving for Loyola College, March 1963. With him are Sugadha and their father.

When I landed at Madras Airport, which was absolutely chaotic, Chechy, Uncle Sreedharan and Aunty Ravamma were waiting for me. They hurried me away and Chechy asked me what I would like to drink. As usual, I asked for a Coke and they all looked at me and said, "There is no Coke here." India had her own local drinks, like mango juice but no Coke. I was thinking to myself, "What sort of country is this without Coke?" Anyway, I decided to have whatever was available. It was equivalent to drinking coloured sugar water.

I settled into my guardians' home and Chechy returned to New Delhi soon after that. I waited patiently for news from Loyola College, and subsequently, my application was successful.

As instructed by my parents, I made arrangements to board at the hostel in Loyola College. Student boarders of the hostel were all boys who came from all over India. The college and the hostel were managed by Jesuit priests; there were very few civilian lecturers. I was assigned to share a room with a boy who came from a distant village. He was a very humble person with a great desire to achieve as it was an honour for him to be able to study at Loyola College. In no time, we became friends. He admired the way I spoke English because his English was very poor. This was because the main language for him at school back home was Tamil. I often helped him with his English papers.

Loyola College then comprised 600 students. The school was managed with a strong sense of discipline and schedule. One day, an arrogant physical education instructor, who was trained in the United States and had acquired an American accent, ordered all 600 of us to assemble at the school field. After putting us through a mass exercise regime, he said, "If any of you can run ten laps around this field, I will take my hat off to him but if anyone can run 20 laps around this field, I will hang myself. You all look very soft and I am very sure that none of you will ever be able to make it."

My newfound friends knew that I was a long distance runner. One of them said, "Do it. Show this fellow once and for all." Determined to prove the instructor wrong, I agreed. I started running and pacing myself and after the tenth lap, I felt that I was able to continue running. The whole of Loyola College was there to watch and cheer me on. Upon reaching the 20th lap, to my surprise some of the students were there to lift me up and carry me on their shoulders. A few of them produced a rope and went straight to the instructor and handed it to him. In chorus, they yelled, "Hang yourself now!" He was very humiliated and stumbled to find the right words in reply. The students shouted at him, "Get lost. Why don't you just return to the States where you are more welcome? You can't even keep your word here." Just to spite him, knowing that he would not do it, students were shouting, "Why don't you just hang yourself?" That one incident made me popularly known to all.

Although I had to live a rigid and disciplined schedule, I tried my best to get used to hostel life. From the very beginning, I was already missing my mother and the friends with whom I grew up. I tried to discipline myself to concentrate on my studies instead of feeling homesick. However, even before I could really adjust to the new environment, I knew that I couldn't stay there as my room was just next to the railway track and the noise from the trains made it impossible to study or sleep. I asked for a change of room but was denied it for they said that the request was received too late. I then decided that I should go and stay in my guardians' house which was not very far from the college. In fact, I could even walk to college.

I went to see the vice-principal to inform him of my intention to move out. He agreed to let me go but said that the college was not refunding the fees for the hostel. He was more interested and concerned about the money. For a better study and sleep environment and my peace of mind, I had no choice but to forego the fees that were paid. Uncle Sreedharan came with his driver, who helped me pack and took me back to his home. Thereafter, I either walked to college, took a cab or was given a ride to college and back by my uncle's driver. It was an arrangement that I liked but my roommate thought I was leaving the hostel because of him. I had to assure him that it had nothing to do with him.

I found studying in Loyola College a bit adventurous. Some of the students could be rebellious and would unite to take up a cause when the situation arose. They joined other universities in rioting and activities like that, in the name of democracy. However, most of the students there were mild and were labelled the slaves of Loyola because we always obeyed orders given to us by the lecturers. I was elected class monitor by the students of my class but the lecturer who was in charge of our class appointed his own family friend's son as the monitor. This did not please my classmates who wanted to protest and make an issue out of it. I advised them against it and said that I was not interested in being a monitor. I convinced them, "Let the person who was appointed be the one. He looks like a decent guy who's embarrassed to be put in a situation like that by the lecturer." He apologised to me and I was happy to tell him to do his duties well.

It was there that I met the nephew of Mr V Manickavasagam Pillai, who was then the Minister of Communications in the Malaysian Cabinet, I think. Manickavasagam's nephew and I became good friends because we were both from this region. He was from Malaysia and I was from Singapore. We spent time together outside of school, having lunch or just hanging out together at my uncle's hotel, Hotel Malabar

Hill. We would have tea there and he would leave for home and I would walk to my uncle's residence.

Generally, the lecturers in Loyola College were very steep in their style of discipline and there was no room for reasoning as far as their rules were concerned. Some of us were not used to such rigid discipline especially if they were unreasonable. There was a Brahmin lecturer who obviously felt full of himself because he was from the highest caste in the Hindu caste system. His general demeanour and attitude towards the students made most of us dislike him for no apparent reason, sometimes. He tied his *veshti* (traditional South Indian wraparound cloth for men) with the tip of one end of the cloth tucked into his back. One day Manickavasagam's nephew and I were simply making a lot of nasty remarks about this man in the Malay language, amusing ourselves at his expense and laughing. Suddenly he turned around and said, "I know a little bit of Malay, too, you know." We were shocked and frightened until he said, "But I have forgotten most of it." Showing it with his thumb and fingers, he added, "A little little, I know." We realised that he didn't know what we were talking about. It taught us one lesson — don't take for granted that others do not know your spoken language.

Not long into the school term, I fell ill with typhoid fever and was confined to my uncle's residence. Later, my guardians decided to put me in Hotel Malabar Hill where the staff could take care of me. I was quarantined in a room with doctors constantly checking on me. When I recovered, I developed a skin condition and had to stay in the same room until I was fully treated for that. I was completely miserable and homesick. It has only been two months since I started school and I was already dreading the whole stay in Madras. I tried my best for my mother's sake but it was getting harder and harder to bear it all. It didn't help with me falling sick.

By the time I recovered, two weeks or more had gone by. I brought the medical certificate to the vice-principal. As usual, the office clerk wanted a bribe before I could see the vice-principal. I scolded and threatened to report him. He was angry with me but also scared, and allowed me to see the vice-principal. I went in and when I showed him the medical certificate he said, "I don't care about the medical certificate. You are fined for being absent for two weeks." I tried to explain that I had been ill all that time but he said, "You should have sent that medical certificate earlier." I was irritated and asked, "How was I supposed to send it earlier when I was given the medical certificate only after falling sick." He responded with, "I am not here to argue with you." His stand was that I did not produce the medical certificate earlier and as such, I should be fined.

I soon came to realise that the entire lecture hall of Loyola College was actually built on the fines collected. I understood immediately their success in collecting money for the building fund. For even the silliest of reasons, they fined students. I asked how much my fine was and if I remember correctly, it was an amount that was not much when you convert it to Singapore Dollars. I took the money and gave it to him. He said, 'Thank you very much. You can go now." I left and said to myself, "This is the last straw. I will not be able to stay in this country and especially in this college. I have to go home."

I sat down to write a long letter to my mother, emphasising my ordeal thus far and how miserable I was. I really wanted to go home. I knew that I should take a boat as the plane fare would cost too much. I was prepared to do that as I could not take the stay any longer.

However, days later, I received a telegram from my father which read, "Come by plane." I showed it to Uncle Sreedharan who said that I should have consulted him before writing to my mother. I felt that there was no point consulting him or anybody else. I had already decided that I was going back. I requested for his assistance to make the arrangements for my departure. He said he would but he informed me that Chechy was coming from New Delhi to Madras to see me before I left.

I notified the principal, Father Sequeira, of my desire to leave and showed him my father's telegram. He approved it and said, "OK, give me five to ten minutes to prepare the school leaving certificate and certificate of good conduct. I'm sorry that you have to leave." I assured him that I was fine with the wait and he was extremely nice because he knew Uncle Sreedharan, too.

After that, out of courtesy, I decided that I should visit the vice-principal to say goodbye. He asked, "Oh, so you are leaving? May I know why you are leaving?" I took the opportunity to say to him, "It's because I can't stand people like you. You are a big bully and you are corrupt. I don't know what you are doing here. You are supposed to be a Jesuit priest but you are a disgrace to your calling." Naturally, he got very angry with me. I said further, "You can do whatever you like, I am leaving." I got into the car, and my uncle's driver drove me back to the principal's office to collect my certificates.

As I was leaving the principal's office and walking towards the car, I saw the vice-principal cycling furiously towards the principal's office. I told him, "I know what you are intending to tell the principal. You are going to tell him not to give me a certificate of good conduct, isn't it? You're too late, old man, because I have already received it. That's the difference when you have a bicycle and I have a car." As I laughed at him, I got into the car and we drove off. On hindsight, I am not proud of myself but then again, I was then a young man, irrational at times. The reason I was very angry with the vice-principal was that he penalised me with a fine for everything and he was constantly picking on me. Well, finally, I had the last laugh.

Two days later, Chechy arrived. She looked at me and said, "You look miserable enough. I'll make the arrangements but before that, please go to Kerala to visit our relatives there. You can see the place where you were born." I agreed.

She gave me my train and air tickets. It was an overnight train journey to Varkala in Kerala State where I stayed with my eldest maternal uncle. It was not really comfortable because there was no modern sanitation but I was glad I went and met my relatives. I even saw the place where I was born. I had no memories of my birthplace as I had left India for Singapore with my parents and my elder sister when I was only five months old. So, it was a strange but warm homely feeling as I looked around the home where my mother grew up in and gave birth to me.

I met my cousins for the first time there. They accompanied me throughout my stay. One of my cousins, Babu, and I cycled to my father's village in Njekkad which was approximately an hour away. We parked our bicycles under a tree and saw a man walking by. Afraid that we might have trespassed into his territory, we asked him if it would be all right to park our bicycles there. He looked at me and realised that I must be a foreigner as I was wearing a pair of jeans. He asked me, "Who are you?" I replied, "I am R Anandan's son." With pride in his voice, he said to me, "Oh, if you stand on your parked bicycle and look, every thing that you see once belonged to your grandfather and your father." I was shocked and said, "Wow, my father was so rich?" He replied, "Yes, but he lost everything because he was in Singapore and when his father and brother died, people came and claimed all the land. He was left with only the land on which you have parked your bicycles." Babu and I laughed at the coincidence.

We walked a short distance and and came upon a house where my father's elder sister lived. As I approached the house, I saw an old lady with thick white hair, still looking very strong, filling a pail of water from the well. My cousin indicated that she was my paternal aunt. I touched the old lady on her shoulder and said, "Do you know who I am?" She said, "How am I going to know who you are? I am an old lady who can't even see properly. So tell me who you are."

I introduced myself to her. Instantly, she hugged me and cried. She said, "At least I have seen you before I die." I felt so pleased that I had made this overnight journey to visit everyone, especially this old aunt. I gave her some money that she refused initially but upon my insistence she took. She gave me a cup of tea and some snacks. We chatted and I could see that she was very delighted to hear my stories about Singapore and kept wanting to hear more from me. Before I left, I told her, "I will come and see you again if I can." She replied, "No son, you will not see me again. Give your father and every one in Singapore my best regards." A few months later, she passed away.

Even now when I think of that old aunt and the way she hugged me and cried, I am filled with tears of the memory. I could feel so much of her love when we hugged as she was so pleased to be able to meet her brother's son. That was very important to her. Babu and I cycled back to Varkala after that visit to Njekkad.

The next day, with mixed feelings but with a store of fond memories, I left Varkala for Quilon where I spent the day with my sister's friend, Dr Santha, in her sprawling house with her big family. The following day I boarded the train and returned to Madras.

One of the highlights of my trip to Varkala, Kerala, was to see the Arabian Sea, and to touch and splash my face with the seawater. I thought, "Now I can go back to Singapore and brag to my friends that I've touched the Arabian Sea."

To a 15-year-old boy, the experience of travelling alone and meeting these people was an eye-opener. I saw so much poverty in Kerala where I was born but despite this, the people walked with dignity. They were clean and their *veshtis* were always crisp and white. However, it was not so in Madras where it was dirty and unhygienic. You'd know that the people had not taken a bath for a long time.

On arrival in Madras, I visited my guardians and spent the night with them. Uncle Sreedharan and the old barber from the hotel, whom I had grown quite fond of, accompanied me to the airport the next day. After I had checked in, the old barber touched me on the shoulder and said, "Come." As he pointed at the International Lounge, he added, "Please take me to that place. I want to have a cup of tea from there. Everytime I come here, I look at the Lounge and wonder when I will ever have a cup of tea there. I will pay for it but you follow me so that I can go in there." This was the year 1963 and rules at the Madras airport were lax. I agreed and accompanied him there for his cup of tea. The tea was served with sugar and milk on the side. He asked, "What is this?" I showed him how he should add the milk and sugar to his taste and mix it. He said to me, "I will always remember you, son. You made my dream come true. I can now tell others that I have been to the International Lounge and had tea!"

Soon after, I bade farewell to both of them and proceeded to clear customs before boarding the plane. A lady before me in the queue was asked to declare the amount of foreign currency in her possession. She said that she had US$500. The customs officer seemed friendly and said to her, "You shouldn't be carrying that much money, you know.

It's illegal. Anyway, it's alright, I will keep mum about it. Just go." She thanked him and moved on.

When it came to me, he asked the same question. I said, "Yes, I have S$20. My mother gave it to me for safe-keeping when I left Singapore in case I needed it for an emergency." He exclaimed, "Oh no, you are not supposed to have this on you. I have to confiscate it." I was annoyed and told him, "If that lady can walk off with US$500, I don't see why I can't leave with S$20. If you want to make a fuss about it, I am going to complain to your superiors and let everyone be checked." He realised that I may have been young but I could not be bullied. Relenting, he said, "OK, you don't have to make a fuss. Just leave." With a feeling of relief, I boarded the aircraft and waited patiently to return home to Singapore.

Unfortunately, my plane was delayed for about eight hours. My friends Choo Poh Leong, Michael Then, Chee San and Tee Kow were waiting for me at Paya Lebar Airport. They were never told that the flight was delayed but they waited for me for almost ten hours! I was overjoyed to see them and I think they felt the same way too, especially after such a long wait. We got into a taxi and went to my home where my parents and younger sister were waiting for me.

The first thing I said when I saw my mother was, "I'm sorry, Ma, but I couldn't do what you wanted me to do. I just couldn't take it." She looked at me without a word. My father said, "You tried to make your mother happy but you couldn't. Now you don't have to make anyone else happy. Just do what you want to do but don't tell me that you want to go to work and that you want to stop studying. You have to continue to study. Find something that you would like to study." I had no choice but to agree. I looked at him and thought to myself, "How lucky I am to have a father like him — so understanding —

always there to give me moral support without criticising me. That made me feel even worse and I had to keep quiet. You know what's running through his mind and you know you have hurt him. You would try to do better the next time.

So I spent the next few weeks hanging around doing nothing because school term had already commenced. I did a lot of reading at home.

By the time I returned to Singapore, it was June 1963. In October 1963, the Naval Base Labour Union decided to go on strike. The Acting Secretary-General of the Union was one Michael Fernandez. I was a curious young boy with nothing to do. I went around to all the centres where the demonstrators were picketing; some of them were my friends who had already started working at the Base. Part of the fun for me was waiting for the free food that was provided by supporters. In the end the Government intervened and said that the strike was illegal. An order was given that everyone had to return to work.

It broke the hearts of so many employees because they had gone on strike for more than 30 days. Everyone had the strength and the resolve to take on the English colonial masters. They were prepared to go all the way with the strike. As it was declared illegal, everyone had no choice but to return to work. Some were sacked and others were warned. My father's bosses were not happy with him and he was afraid that they might also sack him. I heard him talking with my mother late in the night that he might be sacked. I could hear her consoling him, "If that should happen, Subhas will have to go to work until Subhashini comes back as a doctor. Then he can continue with his studies. So don't worry. We will survive." I remember my father saying, "I don't want him to work at such a young age. But if there is no choice, I am sure he will do whatever is necessary." My mother felt assured and said, "We have brought them up in the way that they will always do what is right for us. So don't worry about it."

It was a great relief to finally hear that my father would not be sacked. He was given a warning and he continued to work at the British Naval Base. Michael Fernandez was arrested and locked up with a few others. The days of trade union strikes soon came to an end. Lee Kuan Yew and his government made sure that the trade unions did not get out of hand or have too much power. They succeeded. The trade unions that had leftist leanings were practically closed down and their leaders arrested. Under the watchful eyes of the government, Devan Nair started the National Trade Union Congress which exists till today.

In the start of the new school year in 1964, I was admitted into Raffles Institution to commence Pre-University studies.

I have many friends from all walks of life. Most of them are caring and loyal to our friendship. Of course, there are some 'fly by night' friends. They are there when times are good but disappear when the bad times come. It's painful to realise that in times of trouble or sickness, the people that you think mean so much to you, are not there. They just disappear as though you are suffering from the plague. To me, friendship is more than just saying hello. If you are my friend, I will do practically anything for you, even risking my life, if necessary. I ended up in prison because of my friends. A lot of things happened in my life because of friendship. Many of my friends would have done the same for me but some happen to turn out to be a great disappointment. They are there just to ask you for favours. They are there when you are up and flying but disappear if they feel that your days are done and you are on your way out. Such is life in most situations but having gone through so much in my life, I have learnt to let it all not bother me and to focus on those who really care for me.

TWENTY-EIGHT

MY SOMALIAN EXPERIENCE

I enjoy sharing with my family my visit to Somalia as it was truly an adventure of a lifetime for me. This working trip, where I also went to Rome, opened my eyes to a real world where there is political instability, greed, abuse of power and uncertainty.

It was sometime in 1982, a decade into my practice, that I met an old neighbour called Abdul Rahman who was in the business of timber trading. One day, he came to the office and said he wanted me to vet some documents. Prior to this visit, I had not seen him for a long time. My father used to call him 'Tengku' after the first Prime Minister of Malaysia. We had a long chat, and laughed as we reminisced. I vetted the documents and noted that his office was in CPF Building, within walking distance from my office, which was then in International Plaza. At times I would walk over to his office and have coffee with him or he would reciprocate the gesture. We occasionally went for lunch or dinner together.

One day he asked if I could go to his office. I agreed and there I met someone called Khawi from Somalia. He bought timber from Abdul Rahman quite regularly and this time he wanted help because the Commercial Bank of Somalia had been cheated of a few million dollars by somebody in the Moscow Narodny Bank in Singapore. The Somalian bank had sent their Letter of Credit to purchase rice or some other commodity; the Letter of Credit had been cashed but they never

Subhas (left) with Khawi.

got their goods. The Somalian Government was very angry and contacted Khawi whom they knew visited Singapore regularly.

Khawi asked whether there was anything I could do to help. He said they had already taken action against Moscow Narodny Bank in London. An Anthony Coleman, QC, was acting for them and he asked if I could work along with the QC. I said that I was unable to practise in London. He explained, "No, we want to issue a writ against the bank in Singapore, too, because one of the arguments the Commercial Bank of Somalia had put forward in London was that the whole situation happened in Singapore. So they wish to be ready to institute proceedings against the bank in Singapore."

I was very frank with Khawi and said, "I am not a commercial lawyer. This is too high profile for me. I practise criminal law." He replied, "I know but I think there is an element of crime in this particular incident. Why don't you go through the papers? We will pay you for your services and if we actually have to go to court, maybe you can instruct the QC to come down to argue it." After some thought, I said, "That sounds fair enough."

Khawi gave me all the necessary documents. I looked through them and I told him that this fraud could only be committed with the knowledge of some people in Commercial Bank of Somalia. It was an inside job. He said, "That's what our President thinks. Can you go to Somalia to meet with the President and his ministers to share your thoughts on the matter?" I felt a little apprehensive about having to go to Somalia and said, "That can be done if we meet in London." But he said, "No, you have to go to Somalia." I spoke to Abdul Rahman who assured me that it was a good opportunity; his business in Somalia was increasing significantly.

Khawi had become a friend by then. I agreed to go and it was decided that I should also meet with an Italian shipping company in Italy to negotiate another matter. This company owned ships in Somalia. So in April 1983, I flew to Rome but missed my connecting flight to Viareggio on the west coast of Italy where the company was based. At Rome airport, I was met by Steven, a representative from the shipping company. He asked me whether we could take the train to Viareggio because he wasn't sure when the next flight out of Rome would be. I was keen to get to my destination and agreed to take the train.

Steven got us first class tickets but to our dismay, we found our seats in the private cabin occupied by six middle-aged Italian women. They were really huge and when Steven tried to tell them that the cabin seats were not theirs, they just ignored him. I told him, "Let's not start trouble here. Let's see if we can find some other place." We walked around and there were no empty seats. We walked into the restaurant to have a drink but there were no seats there too. We went back to the open space near our cabin and stood there. It was cold but we had no choice. About an hour before reaching Viareggio, two of the ladies got off. Steven and I quickly sat in the seats they vacated. One of the other two ladies asked where I was from. I said, "Singapore." She didn't seem to know where Singapore was. She then took out a salami sandwich from her bag. She broke it into two and gave me half to eat. I said, "It's OK, thank you very much." She said, "No, I say eat, you eat." I thought, "I'd better eat because I think this woman is capable of creating a scene." Steven told me that if I didn't eat what she had given, it might be considered an insult. I took the sandwich and bit into it. It tasted so wonderful that I wondered why I had been reluctant to accept it. I gobbled it up very quickly. She took a glass, poured some coffee for me and said, "Drink." It was strong coffee but the sandwich and coffee went together. I thanked her and she just smiled.

I spent a day with the shipping company, settling issues under dispute. I returned to Rome the following day to catch my flight to Mogudishu, capital of Somalia. At the airport, I walked from the domestic terminal to the international terminal only to discover that Air Somalia's office, where I was to pick up my ticket, was closed. Wondering what I should do next, I looked around and saw four Americans who asked me if I was also going to Mogudishu. They said they were going there but the flight had been delayed and they didn't know how long it would be delayed. They then asked where I would be staying. By then I had already decided to stay at the Excelsior Hotel in the city. They were staying at the Holiday Inn, which was located near the airport. Before we parted, I said, "We will definitely catch up again." I hailed a taxi and went to Excelsior Hotel. There I rang Singapore and they told me that it was a good hotel as it was near the airline offices.

The next morning I set out to look for the Air Somalia office. All the airline offices were located in the same area. But all the offices, except for Singapore Airlines, were closed as it was Easter. I was wondering what to do while walking back when I saw two policemen riding horses on the main road of Rome. I stood and stared at them as I had never seen such beautiful horses nor had I ever seen policemen on horses before. I watched in awe as they rode past me. Suddenly a Mini Minor car stopped in front of me and a girl shouted something at me in Italian.

I said, "I don't understand you. Can you speak English?" She replied, "Yes, I do. Are you lost?" I told her I wasn't lost and was on my way back to my hotel. She asked if I wanted a ride. At first I thought I'd better not because she could be trouble in so many ways but then I thought, "What the hell! What is there to lose?" I got into her car and thanked her. She dropped me off at the Excelsior which was quite close by and out of courtesy, I asked her if she would like to have breakfast with me. She was surprised that I hadn't had my breakfast yet as it was already mid-morning. Actually, I already had my breakfast. The waiter must have been surprised that I was coming for a second breakfast. He smiled at me. She told me that she could speak English as she was working as an interpreter in one of the embassies. She asked me what I was doing in Rome and I shared with her my dilemma. She said, "I am also stuck here because it's Easter and I can't get a flight to return home to meet my parents." She asked me what I intended to do. I said, "I need to find out when the plane will arrive. In the meantime maybe you could be a tour guide and show me around the city of Rome." She was very obliging and I got a tour of Rome from this girl whom I later bought lunch and dinner, too. I asked her if she could send me to the Holiday Inn near the airport because I thought I might as well join the Americans and leave together with them for Somalia. Very kindly, she took me there.

After checking in, I noticed the Americans were at the Bar. We made our way there. I introduced my new friend to them and one of the guys asked me, "Can I ask her for a dance?" I certainly had no objections. He took her to the dance floor and the other three guys just looked at me and one of them amusingly said, "How did you manage this in just a day?" I told them what happened and they laughed. As she said goodbye, I was grateful that I was not left stranded alone in an unfamiliar city for the whole day. It was a day well spent with interesting company.

The next day, we took the shuttle bus to the airport. There, we waited and waited. Finally, we were told that the plane had not even left Frankfurt; something was wrong with the engine. We went back to the hotel, had our dinner and kept calling Air Somalia. Finally, we were told that the plane might arrive the following morning. They couldn't guarantee us anything but they said that it would be there. In the morning, we went back to the airport and noticed that the Air Somalia office was open. I requested for my ticket. There we waited for the arrival of the plane.

Finally, the plane arrived and when I tried to board it, the Immigration Officer told me that I didn't have a visa. I assured him that my visa was waiting for me at the Somalian airport. He informed me, "The country is in chaos. You can get into a lot of trouble." "Don't worry," I assured him. "I have been waiting here for two days. I must go." "Alright then, you take the risk," he retorted. I proceeded to board the flight.

It was the most horrific plane ride I had ever experienced. Passengers had no regard for seat allocation and sat wherever they liked. Some were even carrying poultry and vegetables. The poultry were flying over our heads. We somehow managed to find a seat each.

It was a ten-hour flight and when I reached Mogudishu, it was nearly midnight. I was told that I had to wait for Khawi's partner, Haji, who was to meet me at the airport with my visa. So the Americans left me while I waited at the airport. I was worried as I did not know who Haji was and whether he would be coming to the airport or not. In the meantime the immigration officers and others were looking at me very suspiciously. I put on a brave front and sat there. Five minutes later, Haji came and apologised to me for being late. He said he had been coming to the airport regularly to find out if the plane would arrive but it was always delayed. That day, he decided to wait at his house, leaving only when he saw the plane descending towards the airport. He spoke to the immigration officer and showed the visa. Obviously Haji was a man who was well respected for they all seemed to be very courteous towards him. He also spoke very good English and I had no problem communicating with him.

He drove me to a hotel for the night. "The whole ground floor is yours," he said. There were only two or three people staying at that hotel. Feeling a little uneasy, as I was supposed to stay at the State Guest House, I asked him, "Why am I staying here?" Khawi had specifically informed him that I needed air-conditioning but apparently the air-conditioner was spoilt and being repaired. Haji said that he would take me there the next day. I had no choice but to agree.

The next morning they took me to the office for discussions and sent me back to the hotel after that. He said he would come again at around 5:00 pm to take me to the guest house. While I was in my room, I heard gunfire and grenade explosions. I grew worried because in Somalia there was always a coup going on. I thought, "Dear God, if there is a coup now, what am I supposed to do?" I heard continuous thundering gunfire. I thought, "I'm not going to die like a rat in my room." It didn't help that the lights were out. It added to my panic. I took my lugguage, walked out and stood on the main road, wondering whether Haji would come for me. My thoughts were on what I should do if nobody came to pick me up. Alone in a strange country in a strange hotel with gunfire and explosions going on — it was quite nerve-wrecking.

I waited for 15 minutes before a car approached me. It was Haji and the driver with somebody else. They greeted me and as usual apologised for being a bit late. It seemed the norm for them to be late.

I took my lugguage, put it into the boot, got into the car and they drove off as though it was just another normal day of activities.

I asked Haji, "Haji, is something happening in the country?" He said, "No, why?" A little perturbed and confused, I said, "Can you hear the gunfire and the explosions?" Casually, he replied, "Ya." Hoping to get a satisfactory response to my confused state, I added, "I thought there was going to be a coup of some sort." He replied, "Oh my God, I'm so sorry. You see, the hotel is near a training firing range for the Somalian soldiers. They were training today with the gunfiring and exploding of grenades. I am so sorry. Were you frightened?" With a sigh of relief, I replied, "Yes, of course. Who wouldn't be afraid?" He apologised to me profusely.

They drove me to the State Guest House, a grand palatial building with security all around. Soldiers were marching along, carrying guns and saluting me as they all knew I was a state guest. An attendant ushered me in with fine hospitality and showed me to my room upstairs. Haji assured me that the State Guest House was safe and well protected. I laughed nervously but with some relief.

The next day, I went to the Commercial Bank of Somalia to meet with the chairman for a discussion. As was the norm in Somalia, the Chairman was late. I had to wait in his office for about three hours. When he finally came, he was apologetic and said he had to rush off again. Feeling anxious as I felt I was being kept in the dark by everyone, I said, "You'd better tell me what is happening. Please answer my questions before you rush off. I am to meet with the President in the afternoon." He looked a bit worried, sat down and tried his best to answer the confidential questions that I asked. I felt a lot more assured of my safety then. Soon after, I was taken to the Palace to meet with Siad Barre, the then President of Somalia, but because of some urgent matter, he could not be at the Palace. I had to leave and return the next day to meet with him. By then, I was quite used to the way the system worked.

I met with the President the next day and he spent about an hour with me, asking for my opinion on the case. I advised him and he said, "Well, do you know what we can do to him if we find out who is creating the problems?" I just kept silent. He authorised me to collect the necessary documents for the Queen's Counsel in London to vet, in order to obtain the QC's advice as to what can be recovered from the situation.

I then went back to the Commerical Bank of Somalia but had to go back again the next day as the Chairman of the Bank was not there. I asked him for certain documents and for an authorisation letter so that I could see the QC and have discussions with him on behalf of the Bank. "Unless I have an authority letter, the QC may not want to talk with me." He agreed and I dictated the letter to his secretary. She started typing but she was such a bad typist and kept erasing the mistakes that there was a hole in the letter. I told her, "Can you just put the paper in for me and I will type it myself?" I used two fingers and typed faster than her with more accuracy and gave it to the Chairman for his signature. I looked at the secretary again. She was a very young and attractive woman and it was obvious that she was not employed for her secretarial skills but for other purposes. After getting the letter signed, I went back to the State Guest House. It was already late in the afternoon. I told Haji, "Please get me on the first plane to London as soon as possible. I want to get out of here as quickly as possible." He replied, "You can't leave tonight as you have to attend a dinner. You will leave tomorrow."

Resigned to my situation, I thought, "Well, I have already wasted so many days here in this God damned country, I might as well spend one more night." Haji and I hung out at the State Guest House with the Chairman of the Bank and a few others — all seven of us — until it was time for dinner. I noticed a few people carrying a roasted camel. They placed it in the centre where we sat. I looked at it, shocked, and exclaimed, "What is this? Camel?" Haji demonstrated to me how to eat it, "Don't try to use fork and spoon to eat this. You have to put your arm right in and pull out everything that you can get with your hand. There is a goat inside the camel and inside the goat are chickens with eggs, potatoes, and rice." I did as he instructed and there in my hand were pieces of camel, goat, chicken, potato and rice. It was a very interesting experience. The spices made it a very sumptuous meal. It tasted wonderful especially the roasted skin of the camel. We ate and although Somalia was a Muslim country, everybody drank whiskey. Eating and drinking merrily was the order of the night. After we had finished, we left the living room for the next group of people to eat. The feasting lasted until all the meat was completely gone. I thought, "This was worth waiting for. It's an experience I will never get anymore."

The next day, before I boarded the flight to Rome, I was handed a briefcase of cash to be delivered to the Bank's London representative for legal expenses. Mogudishu was very warm but when I reached Rome, the weather was very cold, -1 degree Celsius. I was totally unprepared for the change of weather but got used to it after a while.

On arrival in London, I was questioned by the immigration officer about the purpose of my visit. I produced the letter of authority from the Bank and identified myself as their Counsel. He wanted to know if I had sufficient funds to stay in London for a week. I produced my credit cards which he was not satisfied with. So I opened the briefcase that was to be handed to the Bank's London representative. In it was £50,000. He said to me immediately, "Please shut the case. With this kind of money, you can stay in Buckingham Palace."

TWENTY-NINE

A SON'S PROMISE

In my first book I mentioned the promises that people made and the promises I kept. This reminds me of a situation between my father and me.

My father suffered a heart condition and he was on a strict diet of food and drinks. But as with most old Indian men, he loved his whiskey once in a while and we all knew that. One day, a client of mine gave me a special whiskey — old vintage — which I brought home for him. At that time he had just recovered from an angina attack. When I gave it to him, his eyes lit up. I said to him, "Acha, this is really good whiskey. You must have a peg of it." With total glee and delight, he replied, "Of course, I must."

This was some time in 1984 and at that time, Chechy, being a medical doctor, commented, "Stop it! You are not giving him anything like that to drink." I replied, "Why not? He's getting old and being in his twilight years, why can't you allow him to enjoy a shot or two of this good whiskey?" She was adamant and firm in her belief and said, "No, he might not just die but suffer a stroke that could cause him to be bedridden in a vegetative state for a long time. If that happened, are you going to be responsible for his suffering?"

My father and I looked at each other and I saw the disappointment on his face. With much bravado, I assured him, "Have a drink. If anything happens to you, I will make sure that you do not suffer. You know what I mean?" Looking at my facial expression, he said, "Oh, if you promise me that, then I will have a drink." He called his neighbour and they both sat and enjoyed a peg or two. He was so elated taking a sip and exclaimed, "I have never tasted any whiskey as smooth as this!" Everyone at home laughed except Chechy. She didn't think it was funny.

Two or three weeks later, my father had another heart attack and this time it was quite serious. He went into a coma. He was first taken to the old Toa Payoh Hospital at Toa Payoh Rise and later transferred to Tan Tock Seng Hospital. He was not conscious and a ventilator was keeping him alive. We did not know for how long more he was to lie in that state. I knew what was running through Chechy's mind and that of the other members of my family but Chechy, being the great sister she is, put her arm round my shoulder and said, "You are not to be blamed for this. You know that this has had to happen sooner or later whether he drank the whiskey or not."

I felt consoled and I went to see him every day wondering what I should do for him. Do I keep the promise I had made earlier to him? Sometimes when the machines supporting him beeped because his heart had stopped, they would inject medication right into his heart that would get his heart pumping again. I watched this and thought to myself, "Why are they doing this? This man is in a coma. Why do you want to keep him alive?" Nobody seemed to know why it had to be done. I supposed at that time, the law was such that there were no living wills or directives.

Day by day I watched my father lying there in the hospital bed, motionless, being supported by machines that were pumping and beeping all day long. I was drowning in mixed emotions and in a dilemma. Obviously, I could not discuss this moment with him and it was a decision I had to make — a promise I had made to my father. It was hard watching him lie there waiting for his time to go.

I asked the doctors if there was any improvement and if there was any hope of improvement. They were helpless and explained that he was in a very deep coma. I asked, "Why are they keeping him alive then?" Nobody could give me an answer to that. I asked Chechy and she said that he was in a coma and had a slim chance of recovery. I wondered why they were making all the effort to keep his heart beating and keep him alive. She said that it was their duty to keep him alive. They had to provide him with all the opportunities to recover. I could not understand it as this would only mean that he would be lying there motionless for an indefinite time.

It had already been seven or eight days since he lapsed into a coma. I called my friends and asked that a few of them accompany me to the hospital the following night because I wanted them to keep watch while I switched off the ventilator and other equipment. I wanted to ensure that he passed on peacefully.

They looked at me in disbelief and asked, "Do you really want to do that? Will you be able to live with it? You will get into trouble." Feeling very sad and troubled at my father's situation, I said, "I can live with it. I just don't want to see him linger on like this indefinitely. I made a promise to him to do what is necessary so that he doesn't have to lie in this state and I have to ensure that I keep that promise regardless of the consequences." My friends were apprehensive but they understood how I felt and said they were there for me. I assured them, "If I get caught, I will not involve any of you. I just need some moral support from you guys to be there for me." They said that they knew that and were not afraid. They were prepared to go with me to the hospital.

We planned to go the following night at around 10 pm. I went to sleep that night with mixed feelings. Next morning, Chechy rang and said, "Subhas, father is gone. I have arranged for the casket company to take him for embalming and you do whatever is necessary at home to make sure that when he comes back, everything is in order." I assured her that it would be done and asked Choon Kee, the tentage supplier of most of Sembawang then, to pitch up a tent in our compound. We informed all close friends and family.

While waiting for his coffin to be brought home, I sat down on the sofa and thought, "Acha, even in your time of death, you were thinking of me and saving me from an irreversible situation with consequences that could have changed my life. You made sure that you spared me the agony of the promise I made to you."

When the coffin arrived, I looked at the old man and thought, "How much I have owed you and could not pay you back because you have just died on me. From now on, I will not make irrational promises."

We cremated him in the evening the same day. I was proud to see that despite the short notice of his death, through word of mouth, there were hundreds of people present to mourn his loss. I had to conduct the last rites as the eldest son together with my two younger brothers. It was heart-wrenching to complete the ritual and walk on without turning back for a last look at him. I walked straight to my car, sat down and started crying. I sobbed continuously. I did not know whether it was tears of sadness or tears of relief or tears of joy because my father was not suffering anymore but I was overcome with emotion and lots of tears. It had finally sunk into me that I had just sent off a great man.

From top left: Subhas with his father, 1956;
with parents, 1977, and with his mother
at their home in Kampong Wak Hassan, 1982.

THIRTY

MY BELOVED MOTHER

Ten years after my father's death, my mother was admitted to Alexandra Hospital where Chechy was working. She didn't want to be admitted into the 'A' Class Ward, where she would get a single-bedded room, because she had always wanted someone beside her. She insisted on a 'B' Class Ward or the General Ward.

I said to her, "Ma, people will think that your children are stingy and they don't care about you." Her reply was, "Son, whatever they may think is not important. Isn't your mother's comfort more important?" Of course, I agreed and we admitted her to the General Ward as she didn't want the air-conditioning as well.

She was diagnosed with advanced stage cancer. She also suffered a heart attack. She stopped talking for some reason and would just smile in response to whatever we told her. We knew that she was suffering a lot of pain. Chechy and her colleagues made sure she had sufficient morphine to ease her pain but it was not enough. I knew she was in agony under her comforting smiles. She knew how upset and anxious we were and she tried very hard to shield us from her suffering. It was painful to watch her in agony. I felt that I couldn't let her go as I still had so much to repay her for her unconditional love and affection.

I recalled the days when she would sit up reading a book just to keep me company while I studied through the nights. She used to pray for me constantly especially when I was remanded in prison.

I was told that she practically lived in our prayer room. Even when she was confined to a wheelchair in her later years, she would visit me in the hospital when I was ill. I looked at this woman and prayed, "God, why do you make this woman suffer? She is such a loving and giving person, generous to a fault. She prays to you everyday. She has done no evil and I still see her maintain her devotion to You."

Late one night, I had this urge to go to the hospital to see her. I drove to the hospital just in time to see her lying awake in bed, perspiring profusely for some reason and I could see that she was in tremendous agony. I felt helpless and asked her, "Ma, are you alright?" She smiled at me without saying a word. I held her hand and asked her, "Do you need anything?" Once again, she just smiled. I was getting anxious and said to her, "Look, Ma, your children are in a position to give you anything you need. We can afford things that we could not afford earlier. Is there anything that you want?" Again, she just smiled at me with peace in her eyes.

Suddenly, she motioned me to bend towards her and she then hugged me tightly. I cannot remember her ever hugging me at all. Although it was comforting when she hugged me, I thought, "Why is she hugging me now?" I felt maybe she was saying goodbye and before I could break into tears, I held her hands and said to her, "I'll see you tomorrow, Ma."

As I walked away, something told me that I would not see her alive the next day. I got into the car and as I was heading for home, I broke down and cried because I felt that that was the end. I felt happy, too, that I had had this sudden urge to visit her and got a hug from her. I prayed to God for his compassion: "Dear God, please let her go peacefully. Don't let her suffer anymore." Only then did I realise that I was ready to let her go. When I reached home, I shared with Vimi the warm and touching moment I experienced with my mother. She nodded her head and comforted me.

The next morning, I went to the office as usual. An hour later, I received a call from Vimi telling me that the family was rushing to Alexandra Hospital and that we should be there too for we may be losing our mother. When we got there, she was already unconscious and her heart rate was dropping. We took turns to hold her hand and said our goodbyes. We stood there watching as her heart rate dropped and with her last breath, her heart finally stopped. It was a moment of reality that was hard to bear but I was relieved that she was no longer in pain.

Chechy arranged for the casket company. She is emotionally the strongest amongst us, very stoic and composed in times of crises. I rang up my friends to inform them of her death and to make arrangements for tentage for the wake because we were told that we would not be able to obtain a slot on the same day for her cremation. When I reached home, I saw that the tentage, chairs and tables were already there.

After what seemed like a lifetime, although it was a few hours, my mother's coffin arrived eventually. We placed the casket in the living room and I was surprised at the number of people who came to pay their last respects to her. I saw friends and relatives whom I had not seen for years. They came because this woman was special to all of them. The next day when she was taken for cremation, and I, as the eldest son, had to again conduct the last rites with my two younger brothers. After that I walked to my car but this time I did not cry. I think all the tears had been shed earlier, when I was praying and hoping desperately for her recovery. In reality, I was glad that her suffering was over. I thought of all the good memories I shared with her and took comfort in them.

THIRTY-ONE

SLIPPER MAN'S CHINA BRIDE

I am approaching the end of my book. I have one or two more cases to share. One is the case of a Chinese bride, Wu Yun Yun, who was forced by her parents to marry Tan Lead Shake, a politician from an opposition party.

Wu came, reluctantly, to Singapore in 2001 when she was 19 years old as her parents had already collected a dowry from Lead Shake's father. She had to live with an extended family which included her husband's parents, an unmarried older brother-in-law and another brother-in-law, Tan Lead Sane, who was also married to a Chinese, Huang Mei Zhe. This couple was in a very loving relationship whereas Wu and her husband were not. Wu claimed that he was cold towards her. It was also obvious to her that her mother-in-law, Madam Ng Bee Hion, was fond of Huang and always treated her better. This began from the very moment she moved into the house after marriage and over a period of time, it grated on her emotionally and she festered resentment for the both of them. She was filled with jealousy and resentment, and started harbouring ill thoughts including thoughts of killing them.

Wu would take breaks, with or without her husband, and return to her hometown in China with her two children to be with her family. Her father was not happy when she stayed long and she felt very isolated as quite often he would insist that she return home to her husband immediately. This absence of love and understanding from her loved ones sent her spiraling down into deep depression triggered by the lack of love and sense of belonging as she felt mentally alone in both homes.

Finally, one day in June 2008, she got so riled up that it unleashed a violent irrational person in her. She bought a knife and stabbed her sister-in-law, Huang, in her neck while she was asleep with her own husband, Lead Sane. Huang yelled and woke up her husband. When he sat up, Wu lunged the knife twice into his chest and once into his abdomen. Sadly, Lead Sane died in hospital. In a state of panic, Wu ran downstairs, collected some belongings and ran towards the main gate of the house to escape. She failed to open the gate as she had forgotten the passcode then. Her mother-in-law Madam Ng tried to stop her and was injured by her as well. Wu ran to the back of the house, climbed over the back gate and ran away. Her husband, Lead Shake, was totally helpless and did not know how to reach her. When she contacted him and said that she wanted to see him, he arranged a meeting and called the police. Wu was arrested and charged with murder and attempted murder. However, due to her deep depression and diagnosis of major depressive disorder, her charges were reduced to culpable homicide and she was sentenced to jail.

This case brings out how human beings can react when they feel that they are unfairly treated. Jealousy can lead to violence.

When she was first charged, Wu had no counsel. Her family was very poor. Her father and sister arrived from China and stayed at a cheap boarding house. Mr Wu was advised by the media that he should look for me to help his daughter. He managed to seek me out and pleaded desperately for help. When he told me of his plight as a father and that he needed my help, I had to agree. I read through the notes of the case and agreed with her family. Wu's sister, who accompanied their father, pleaded with me to help them and they were very grateful that I was willing to take on the case.

People wonder why I took this case up. Like all my cases, I believe that Wu should be given the best defence. The fact that she is poor or that she's from China did not in any way affect my conviction to help. She needed my help and I felt especially for her family who were desperate to seek assistance. It made me feel even more for Wu's family and the consequences that drove her to this state.

We went to court and mitigated for Wu. As she was diagnosed with major depressive disorder and qualified to plead diminished responsibility of her actions, her charges were reduced from murder and attempted murder to culpable homicide. She briefed me on how she had been treated from the time she married into the Tan family. Justice Kan Ting Chiu was kind enough not to give her life imprisonment which the prosecution had asked for. Instead, he handed out a total sentence of 16 years for both the charges. The attempted murder of her mother-in-law, Madam Ng, was taken into account.

We visited her occasionally in prison because she had no visitors in Singapore. Eventually, she got used to prison life and she herself said that she did not want to bother us anymore. She was very grateful for our help but convinced us that she would manage. We understood.

Her sister visited us again and asked if we could arrange for her to serve sentence in a Chinese prison. I explained to her that there were no such reciprocal arrangements between the countries and I told her that her sister would be more comfortable in a Singapore prison than any Chinese prison. I advised her to leave the matter as it is. With good behaviour Wu should be released in ten years' time or less.

I've described in this book a few cases that stemmed from acts of passion. These are not the only cases that I've handled. There are many more such cases. All these cases show that human beings are naturally compassionate — some of us just do not want to admit it. Simply put, some do not want to show their softer side.

Personally, I too have pretended not to care but I know that is not my true self. I care for people and I care for their problems. I think, initially, I did not want to get involved because I was afraid of the hurt it would cause me. However, a time will come when you look around and you see so many people doing good and you tell yourself, "You have to start thinking about others besides yourself. If you can help, you must help."

I sometimes ask my son, "Are you going to be a lawyer?" I would tell him that he could earn a lot of money from practising law, especially corporate law and if in the right firm, but if he were to go into practice just to make money, then the motives are not right. In my opinion, when you go into law, you are in a position to help others — especially those who are not as fortunate as you are. Do not turn away from them. Help them. You will find that you get better satisfaction from that than from what the money can bring you. Most often, we want our children to be successful professionals. I look at my son and I think that it doesn't matter what his calling is but I want him to be a good human being who will have compassion for his fellow beings.

I shared this with a reporter once and he looked at me and said, "I have put this question to so many people and they have all wanted their children to be lawyers, engineers or some kind of professional. You are the first one to give this answer."

THIRTY-TWO

EVERY CRIMINAL DESERVES A DEFENCE

The other case I would like to mention is the case where a taxi driver, Lim Ghim Peow, poured petrol on his ex-lover, Mary Yoong Mei Ling, and set her on fire. He had been very angry and frustrated with her as she did not want to take him back and was on the verge of marrying someone else, and so he decided that he had to teach her a lesson.

He went to where she stayed and poured petrol on her before setting fire to her using his lighter. She suffered third degree burns and eventually died. It was a painful death. The prosecution wanted to charge him for murder for they believed that it was cold-blooded murder — premeditated. But they found that he was suffering from major depressive disorder and had been suffering this disease for some time, and not that it came about suddenly after the incident.

My assistants, Sunil and Diana, conducted the mitigation plea because I was ill. The newly promoted judge, Justice Tan Siong Thye, decided to sentence the accused person to 20 years' imprisonment. The prosecution had asked for 16 to 20 years; we had asked for ten to 12 years. Our client was given 20 years as the Judge was of the view that he got off lightly and was not charged for murder which would have resulted in a death penalty.

When I returned to the office (I was not on dialysis that day), Sunil and Diana informed me that they had filed an appeal. They felt

Subhas with his trusted team. From left: nephew Sunil,
Diana Ngiam and Sandra Cheng, Subhas' longtime
personal assistant and friend.

that 20 years was too long. Sunil told me that it would be good if
I could take the case, although we were doing the appeal pro bono
because the taxi driver's family was unable to pay the fees. So we did it
pro bono as we believed that he should not have been given 20 years.

The hearing of the Appeal came up in July 2014. By this time,
after months of recuperation from my near-death ordeal at the end of
2013, I felt like I was ready to take on some cases at the office. It was
a very encouraging feeling and my drive to work was revved up once
again.

When I appeared before the Court of Appeal, Justice of Appeal
Chao Hick Tin welcomed me and said that it was very good to see
me back in court. Justice Andrew Phang said that I could remain

seated while arguing the case instead of having to stand to argue. I was touched by his kind gesture but decided that it would be rude to sit and conduct my case in the highest tribunal. Anyway, we lost the Appeal and the Court of Appeal agreed that the Trial Judge had meted the sentence to reflect the gravity of the offence and they believed that 20 years was not manifestly excessive.

I went up to the accused person who was sitting in the dock and told him that we had lost the appeal. He knew and understood what the judges had said but he said that he was very grateful to me for coming down to argue his case for him. His family thanked me similarly and said that they would never forget that although I was unwell, I argued the appeal. I was quite touched by their gratitude.

THIRTY-THREE

THE YELLOW RIBBON OF HOPE

A good friend of mine, Noor Mohamed Marican, is currently the President of the Association of Muslim Lawyers (AML). He has always been very supportive and encouraging of my passion towards giving ex-inmates a second chance in life. The Yellow Ribbon Foundation was set up for this purpose. Marican was very keen to set up a bursary award in my name, something that I was not in favour of and felt awkward about, especially when he suggested organising an event called "A Tribute to Subhas Anandan".

As I said earlier, pro bono work has always been a part of my practice since 1971 when I was called to the Bar. It is something I enjoy doing. It is part of my legal practice and I don't see the need for any sort of recognition. When the Yellow Ribbon Foundation was set up, I was very pleased to know that the establishment was concerned for the well-being of the ex-inmates, something that really bothered me as I often hope not to receive a visit from an ex-client who has committed another offence. I feel that a lot of them are lost when they are released and there is not enough family or society support for them. They tend to go astray again easily. So the intention of the Yellow Ribbon Foundation is a noble one and I am very supportive of it.

The discussion with Marican in regard to setting up a bursary award in my name ended as part of a casual conversation in passing and I didn't mention it to Vimi or any other family member as I didn't see the need for it. Three days before the actual event though, Marican informed me that it was being organised and in fact, had been publicised in the AML's *Al-Mizan* periodical for October 2014. I had given an interview that also appeared in the same issue. I had no choice but to let Vimi know about the event.

We were just sitting around that particular evening, chatting and reminiscing about the past, something I seem to do quite often these days. I said to her, "You know what? Marican has organised a tribute for me. Some kind of bursary award under the Yellow Ribbon Foundation for ex-inmates." She noticed that I seemed uncomfortable about it and asked, "Are you OK with it? It seems like you don't want it. You'd better let him know." I told her, "It's all set. It's in three days' time, on 28 October 2014." She exclaimed, "So soon? So how? Don't we need to invite family and friends for their support?" I was at a loss. I didn't know how to answer her as I felt it was just too short a time to let anyone of them know. She whipped out her mobile phone and said, "No worries, I will send a mass text to all in my contact list." Not long after that, she was inundated with replies and most of them were excited and agreed to attend the tribute despite the short notice. That really warmed my heart. I realised we do have very good family and friends around us.

A copy of the AML's October *Al-Mizan* was handed to me and there it was, right at the back under "Upcoming Events", "A Tribute to Subhas Anandan". I noticed that the Guest of Honour was Mr K Shanmugam, Minister for Law and Foreign Affairs. It was definitely something that was of importance.

I was still filled with mixed feelings about the event. On the evening of the tribute, I was overwhelmed to see my family, close friends,

The October 2014 edition of *Al-Mizan*.

colleagues at the Bar as well as members of the Bench mingling with one another. Even the former President of Singapore, Mr SR Nathan, was present. I was truly touched and felt that it was, after all, a good closure to my legal practice as I had already harboured thoughts of retirement. I had plans to focus on giving talks at schools to encourage students to do better in life as individuals and to give back to society. I have always felt that a lot of them lacked proper guidance at home and tend to become wayward easily. For those who had been punished for their offences, I always hoped that they would be given a second chance to live their lives better.

HERE ARE EXCERPTS FROM AN INTERVIEW WITH SUBHAS CONDUCTED
BY THE EDITORIAL TEAM OF *AL-MIZAN*, PUBLISHED IN OCTOBER 2014.

Al-Mizan: Good afternoon, Subhas, it is our honour to be able to conduct this interview with you. Can you share with our readers how your family has supported you since the start, throughout all the difficult, life-threatening times that you have gone through? In particular, we are sure that your wife, Mdm Vimala Kesavan, has played a major and irreplaceable role in your life thus far.

Subhas: I must start by saying that, in many ways, my wife changed my life. Before I met Vimi, I lived life by the day and never planned for the next day. I was very carefree and gave my money away to people who never gave it back to me. I spent what I earned. When she came into my life, she helped me to set aside money for savings and gave me financial stability. She managed all my affairs for me and helped me. On top of that, and more importantly, she provided me with emotional stability. We were dating for over nine years before she married me.

I had my first serious heart attack before our marriage. I remember being in hospital, paralysed with loss of speech. This was in 1978, and everybody told me to retire. You know, my sister actually told my friends to pray for me to die, because if I recovered I would be paralysed on my right side. When Vimi came to visit me at the hospital, I remember telling her that she should leave me. She is about 10 years younger than me. Why would anyone want a paralysed man who cannot speak? But she looked at me and shook her head. That was all.

After that, slowly, I recovered and we got married. She was very understanding and tolerant. She is truly my pillar of strength. She has contributed so much to what I am today. Even my book, which was a bestseller for 18 to 20 weeks, she was the one who transcribed and corrected every page of it. Every major thing that I did in my life, my wife had a role to play, and she continues to support me everyday.

Al-Mizan: That is truly a touching and beautiful love story. Speaking of your health, we understand that you've had a few near-death experiences. What gave you the strength to recover and fight back each time?

Subhas: The last time when I fell extremely ill was in December 2013. In January 2014, the doctors told my wife to take me back and arrange for home care because I was going to die. They wanted me to comfortably pass on at home. Vimi and my elder sister, who is a doctor, refused to listen. I think what made me recover was the strength that my wife, son, siblings and close friends gave me. They were there all the time, praying for me and praying for the best.

I remember my younger sister coming into the ICU and holding my hand as I lay on the hospital bed. She asked me, "Big brother, do you want to live?" I kept quiet as I didn't know how to respond. She asked me again, "Do you want to live?" I asked her why. She replied that everyone could pray for me; in fact, our friends and relatives from all over the world, with different faiths, were praying for me. But she said all the prayers wouldn't help if I didn't want to fight for my own life. That really made an impact on me and I said yes, I do want to live. Then she looked at me and said, "You will be okay." True enough, I did recover.

Honestly, at that time, I didn't know that if I recovered, I would have to go for dialysis three times a week. But on hindsight, even if I had realised that, I would still have made the decision to live. I remember my younger sister asking me, "Don't you want to see your wife, your son graduating, your niece getting married, and Sunil having children?" I would still have chosen to live because of that.

Al-Mizan: **Many of us can't imagine going through such experiences. What is the biggest takeaway that you have gained from them?**

Subhas: All the so-called successes that one may have are nothing compared to the love one has from his family. That is the most important thing. A close-knit family is so important, especially in times of crisis. I am so blessed to have a close-knit family. There are many families who are like strangers to each other. It was after going through such an experience that I knew that when I recovered, I definitely wanted to spend more time with my family and close friends.

You know, I was so touched. Friends whom I hadn't seen for years came to the hospital to console my family when they heard about my ill health. I think I got all my priorities wrong before my sickness; it was all about work and I had so little time for my family and friends. All of a sudden, it just hit me! Life is so unpredictable. Now, I call my friends who are far away more often.

Many people have come forward to tell me that I've reached the top of the ladder, that I am the most popular criminal lawyer in Singapore. So what? You can be everything but if you don't have the love of your family, you have nothing. That is why I have immense respect for the Malay community, which has very bonded families. When I was in hospital, my sisters told me that there was an old Malay lady in the ICU, which was why the ICU area was crowded. You see, the whole *kampong* was there. As a patient, when you see your relatives and friends coming to visit you, I can tell you personally that it gives you a lot of courage and confidence. I have noticed this amongst the Malay community. They are always willing to visit and cheer a person up. That is very nice especially when you are sick.

Al-Mizan: **Could, you share with our readers a few of your near-death experiences and what went through your mind during these experiences?**

Subhas: I will talk about three of these experiences, not because I only had three, but because I remember these three very well. If I recall correctly, I have been to the brink of death at least five times.

When I had my first heart attack in 1978, I was paralysed. I was very frightened because I didn't want to live with my right side paralysed and I definitely didn't want to lose my ability to speak. I thought that I would rather die. What went through my mind? A lot of things. There were many things that I thought I should have done but had not done. To be honest, I told myself that in the future, I would do this and that, but after I recovered, I forgot about what I had told myself. I am trying not to repeat it this time around. My recovery was slow but I thanked God for letting me get better without any defects. I do still have slight slur of speech but I am so happy that I survived that incident.

The other significant experience I went through was my heart failure in 2008. Vimi had gone for a cruise. One day I started coughing but I still went to work. I was in KhattarWong then, and after work I went with my colleagues for a drink near Harry's Bar. I was very tired when I got home and my cough had worsened. Vimi returned home that day and heard me coughing. She dropped her suitcase at the door and asked me what had happened. When I told her about my day, she immediately said that I had to go to the hospital. I told her there was no need and that I just had to rest well that night. Thankfully, she didn't listen to me and called my elder sister, who was off-duty that day. My sister called her colleague in Alexandra Hospital and told Vimi to take me there. My elder sister said that she would also join us there. My wife and son immediately took me to the hospital. I remember the doctor saying that my heart had failed and that my lungs were full of water. The hospital staff told Vimi that I would have died had I gone to the hospital just a bit later, because I wouldn't have been able to breathe. That was when I suddenly realised how serious it was.

The other occasion was in April 1990, when Vimi was pregnant with our son. He was going to be born in June. I had pain in the bladder due to some stones. I went to Singapore General Hospital. They gave me an epidural and removed the stones. It's not really a complicated procedure and I was supposed to go home the next day, but that evening I was screaming in pain. I was drinking so much water! The doctor touched my stomach, which had become tender and very painful. My blood pressure was also going up very high. The doctors were all worried that my heart would give up, and they said that I had to go for surgery. My elder sister called the head of the hospital who came and spoke to me. She said that there was a good chance I wouldn't recover from the surgery with my heart and blood pressure in that condition, but still the surgery had to be done. I said OK.

My friends were there at that time. I remember telling them that I didn't want my son to grow up without the love of a father. I told them that they would be my replacement and would have to help me look after him, if I passed on. I told Vimi that I was not ready to go yet, but if I did, she did not have to worry as everything would be taken care of. The only thing was that I would be sad that I was unable to see my son before passing on.

The anaesthetist in charge of my procedure was my sister's good friend. She made the decision that the surgeon had to put some machine into my body. She said that my lungs would never clear unless the machine was put in. She told me that there was a 50 per cent chance that I might die in the operating theatre, but that she would do everything possible to keep me alive, including using a ventilator. She told the surgeon that she would take full responsibility if anything happened to me. She then came to my room, held my hand and asked me if I was a risk taker. I said yes, and I would follow her advice and go through with it. In the end, I didn't even have to use the ventilator. I survived, my blood pressure went down, and I could go home after I was discharged. You see, what I learnt is that you have to take risks and have faith sometimes.

Al-Mizan: **Many people see you as a fighter. You have fought hard, not only for your survival through such experiences but also for the underdogs in society, for accused persons who would have had the benefit of legal representation otherwise. Have you made many enemies in the process?**

Subhas: To me it doesn't matter if you make enemies because of your profession or the principle you believe in. If an underdog deserves a defence, I will give it. Even if an accused person has committed heinous offences, I will represent him. If I make people angry in the process, so be it. I have received death threats and people telling me they will kill me so many times. People even ring up my secretary and tell her to tell the boss that he will die. At the end of the day, as Gandhi said, only the strong can forgive. I don't hold grudges against people. Those days are gone. I am strong and have forgiven them. But just because I have forgiven them doesn't mean that I have to be associated with them. We each lead our own lives.

Al-Mizan: **You have been in practice for over 40 years now. When you first started, what kind of goals did you set for yourself? How do you view these goals today?**

Subhas: I was called to the bar in January 1971. I had many idealistic goals then and I carried these goals from university into practice. I was the secretary-general of the Socialist Club in university. I was questioned in a Select Committee Hearing about my socialist activities, and they even called me a pro-communist. I said no, I was a leftist. I believed that everybody is equal and I guess many things were in a way similar to communist ideals.

When I started practice, people like me wanted to make right what we thought was wrong through law. But after a few years, we found out that our ideals and what we saw in real life were two very different things. It is all well and good to be an idealist, but you have to be practical. If you think about it, what we were advocating was actually not fair; as it was tantamount to saying that the person who doesn't work is entitled to take from a rich person who is working hard. The equal distribution of wealth cannot be fair if each person is not pulling his weight. We were not in Camelot any more. Not many goals could be achieved. But what was fair was that we managed to help a lot of people who couldn't afford lawyers. We gave them a chance and we fought for the amendment of laws which we thought were unfair.

All my life, I have been fighting for fair and equitable criminal justice. As time went on, I felt that the law was so lopsided. The prosecution had all the advantages such that, sometimes, I feel that on the side of the defence, we are fighting blindfolded. Of course, things have changed since I started practice. Many of us advocated for amendments to make certain things fairer. To a certain degree, I am proud to say we succeeded. The Criminal Procedure Code was amended. The Penal Code has also changed. It may not have levelled the playing field, but some amendment is better than none. Of course, more can be done, and there will be changes for the better hopefully.

One of the most important things that I have always hoped to see is the abolishment of the mandatory death penalty. Don't get me wrong. I am not against the death penalty. In fact I do believe it is necessary for certain offences. I have been criticised for saying that, but it is my belief. When you rape and kill a young girl, or cause women or children to die, for certain offences, why should society keep you in jail and feed you? But in my opinion, the death penalty should not be mandatory. Let the judge decide. The judge is well-placed and more than capable to make the decision whether a person deserves the death penalty. Let the judge have the discretion. Another thing I truly hope to see in my lifetime is for every accused person to be accompanied by a competent lawyer in court, whether he can afford it or not.

Al-Mizan: **Did you ever consider entering politics?**

Subhas: I was interested in politics at one time. Like I said, we were so idealistic after university and thought we would change the world. Unfortunately for me, I was not a citizen then. I was born in India and came to Singapore when I was five months old. I was stateless till 2001. I had to travel with a certificate of identity. If I wanted to go to Johor, I had to get a visa from the Indian High Commission. There was a fear that I would be deported to India when I was in university.

I applied for citizenship in 1972 after I graduated. I was rejected for 10 years. A few years later, I applied again but this time there was no reply at all. I took it that I wouldn't be getting citizenship. Then out

of the blue, they called me when the newspapers reported in 2001 that I was given the Legal Eagle of The Year award by the Law Society. I think the reporter had indicated in the last paragraph that I was still not a citizen of Singapore. Maybe the authorities decided that I should be a citizen after that! They called me up and gave me citizenship soon after. I was given a passport and finally became a citizen in 2002.

Al-Mizan: **If you had been a Singapore citizen in 1971, would you have entered politics?**

Subhas: Yes, and I would have entered the Opposition. I've always spoken my mind, without fear, against or for the government's policies. I believe that in order for Singapore to flourish, we must be fair and unbiased when we judge policies. If a policy is correct, support it. If it is wrong, speak out against it. But don't blindly oppose any policy just because you support a particular political party. We must do our part and engage constructively and positively for the good of our nation.

Al-Mizan: **When you first started practice, you ran your own firm. Since then, you have worked with many different big firms. What are your thoughts on practising in such different working environments?**

Subhas: My happiest moments in practice were when I was running my own firm. I could make my own decisions and work at my own convenience. It was very flexible. Then I formed a partnership with MPD Nair; that was good because he left everything to me as it was just us two lawyers. But of course, when more people joined, things became more complicated. Partners are different human beings with different priorities. That's when I realised a partnership is really not easy.

At that time, Harry Elias Partnership decided to start their own criminal law department. Back then, the larger firms began to form criminal law departments simply because of this: if their corporate client knew a layperson in trouble, and there was nobody in the big firms to do the criminal work, the big firms would have to refer work to the smaller firms; but in the process they risk losing their business. I was asked to join Harry Elias. I was quite tired of running the partnership, so I agreed and went in as a consultant. It was quite refreshing because I didn't have to worry about things like rental and the salaries of my staff. I was there for seven years.

After that, I joined KhattarWong as they were also setting up a criminal department. From there, I joined RHT Taylor Wessing, my present firm. They have been extremely nice and understanding to me, especially considering the state of my health for the past year.

If I could start all over again, I would probably want to be in a small firm for the reasons I mentioned earlier.

Al-Mizan: You have done so much pro bono services in all your years of practice. Please share with us what pro bono was like when you first started and how things have changed since then.

Subhas: Back then, there was no system or programme, unlike how it is now. Each lawyer provided his own pro bono services; we each did not know what the other was doing.

I guess the closest there was to a system was the assigning of capital cases to lawyers in the High Court. That time, there was a register of lawyers, and everybody took turns to do it. Of course, some lawyers who did not practise criminal law would find it difficult. I remember there was a problem when a lawyer did not present the capital case he had been assigned well because the last criminal case he did was probably a bicycle theft 20 years earlier. He tried to tell that to the Registrar, but the Registrar insisted that he had to deal with the case. This was reported in the papers. After that, the system changed and the register only contained names of people who practised criminal law. The chances of criminal law practitioners getting assigned such cases increased but we never complained. We felt it was something we had to do, something we could give, like doing National Service maybe.

Pro bono services now is very different from what it was when I started in practice. I was from a *kampong* in Sembawang. People were poor and could not afford to pay school fees and their children had many problems. I couldn't say no to them due to the *kampong* spirit. We all helped our neighbours, we had a sense of duty to help anyone who was in trouble. We understood each other's problems better because we came from the same *kampong* — it was nothing but genuine compassion. Some of them committed offences not because they wanted to but because they had no choice. They were so poor that they had to steal. They were not hardcore criminals. I tried to help them. They were extremely grateful. Some of them gave my mother gifts such as chickens and eggs. That is how I started my pro bono work to help others some 40 odd years ago.

When we formed the Association of Criminal Lawyers of Singapore (ACLS) in 2004, our main aim was to provide a lot of pro bono services, which we did and continue to do. Our members offer their services quietly and purely for the satisfaction they get from knowing that they are helping somebody in need. They personally don't gain anything and they don't want to gain anything — that's the real value of pro bono. You need to help others without any expectations.

The state of pro bono now is different. The word itself has lost its meaning. Now, there are plans to give some money to lawyers who volunteer to assist. To me, even if you take $5 or $500, it is not pro bono already because you are being paid something. In ACLS we will continue to help people who need our assistance without any expectation of payment. We do it because we want to do it, without any need for publicity or any ulterior motives.

Al-Mizan: **Recently, there has been much discussion in the law fraternity to make pro bono mandatory for all lawyers. The Committee to Study Community Legal Services Initiatives has recommended mandatory reporting of pro bono hours as a start. What are your views?**

Subhas: I have said before that I disagree with this. Pro bono must come from the heart. When people are forced to do pro bono work, it is no longer pro bono. When it is mandatory, some goodwill is taken away and it is difficult to tell who is doing it because of compassion, and who is doing it because he is forced to do it or because he is given some allowance. When you force a lawyer to do a pro bono case, he may not do a reasonably good job because he doesn't like it or isn't used to it. As for the reporting of pro bono hours, there will be difficulties in monitoring and verifying it. The system may lead to abuse. At the end of the day, to me, pro bono must be done with compassion and from the heart, and not through any mandatory policy.

Al-Mizan: **Of late, many people refer to the practice of criminal law and family law as community law. Many lawyers nowadays are reluctant to practise in these areas of law as they feel that these areas may not be financially lucrative as corporate or commercial law. As a criminal law practitioner, what do you think of this?**

Subhas: Of course, an average criminal lawyer would not make as much money as an average corporate lawyer. That has always been the case. However, at the end of the day, it is simply a matter of priorities and satisfaction.

Through criminal law, I get satisfaction, albeit in a different way. When I go to hawker centres, many people come up to me, talk to me and ask about my well-being. When I was very sick, people I didn't even know told me that they were praying for me. Their concern deeply touched me, and to me this is the type of compensation that I get for practising in my field. There are different types of compensation for different fields of law. You can't have everything.

Financially, I am lucky as criminal law has made me neither poor nor rich. I am doing okay. Criminal law has given me a good income and satisfaction which I might not have obtained from practising other areas of law.

Al-Mizan: **After so many years of practice, you must have made many meaningful friendships with your fellow lawyers. Share with our readers some interesting stories about these friendships.**

Subhas: There are so many stories. For example, I have known Noor Marican from the time he started practice in 1975 and we have been good friends for such a long time. We have stood by each other and are both fiercely loyal to one another. He does a lot for ACLS because of his genuine compassion for pro bono work and also, I believe, because of our friendship. We are in fact more like brothers and our relationship is something not easy to find. Even if he becomes some important figure one day, I know that I can always ask him to come over for coffee.

People call him Sammy Davis Jr. because of their resemblance. Once, there was a show; the artiste who was emceeing the show said that she had brought her good friend, Sammy Davis Jr., to attend the show. Everybody clapped happily when the friend appeared, thinking he was Sammy Davis Jr. But it was actually Noor Marican. That was very funny.

He has a wry sense of humour. He is one person who will speak the truth, even if that will cause him to make enemies. To me, that is a virtue I respect. He was always been there for me amidst my many challenges and battles.

Al-Mizan: **What is your advice for young lawyers today?**

Subhas: Law is a difficult profession. You must learn to handle other people's problems very fast. If you are doing criminal law, somebody's life is in your hands and you have to be very disciplined. When you take on a case, whether civil or criminal, you must give 100 per cent, so much so that even when you lose, your conscience is clear and you know that you have done everything possible. If you want to do criminal law, you must have the compassion for it. If you don't have that, it will be very difficult. Young lawyers must accept hard work and not try to cut corners. They should respect the seniors in the profession, be disciplined and competent. When you go to court, be prepared. No judge likes to see an ill prepared lawyer. You must always remind yourselves not to be arrogant just because you have a law degree. To be a good lawyer, you must be honest with yourself. Let your conscience be your guide and you will be all right.

Al-Mizan: On a similar note, personally, do you want your son Sujesh to go down the same route that you have taken?

Subhas: Honestly speaking, I want my son to be a good human. Whether he is a good lawyer or doctor doesn't matter to me. He must have time for people who are not as fortunate as him. I hope he will show the same type of compassion that I have shown to the people who are in trouble. Be helpful, not arrogant. Be there for people. That's all I want him to be.

THIRTY-FOUR

LAST WORDS

I have reached the end of my book. I have said what I have wanted to say without hesitation. I am not going to be very popular with some people. I have to accept the consequences when I have been candid. It really doesn't matter what people think of me. It matters more what you think of yourself. Can you cope with your own hazy conscience or do you cope with some of the things you did very cowardly?

I have been asked to give lectures by institutions. I will accept some and I think my topic this time will be "Never give up", because I feel the younger ones especially tend to give up too easily today. Remember that some of the battles that you fight are never fought alone. There's always family and good friends who will be rooting for you and giving you all the moral support that you need. So never give up. If I had given up, I would not be writing this book. I would have just allowed myself to wallow in self-pity and the rest of the days of my life would amount to nought. I didn't give up simply because I felt that I had a lot more on my plate and I needed to reflect on my life. I wanted to spend more time with my close friends and family. I felt that there were many things that I had to do which I did not.

One of the things that I have to do is to help rebuild my family temple that is in dire need of renovation. I have been associated with the temple for so long that it is a part of me although there were occasions when I lost faith. You have to do what you have to do, that is, to fullfil your obligations and one of my obligations, as the Chairman of the Board of Trustees, is to ensure that the temple is rebuilt properly. In that, I have the assistance of the committee who are mainly comprised of my childhood friends. Even though I feel that some of the members of the committee do not deserve to be there, they're all we have because, as usual, the best never come forward to assist.

I have reached the age of 67 years and it has been a very eventful 67 years. There are many things that I have done that I regret but then a life without any regrets is really not a life, is it?

In my 43 years of practice, I have come across all sorts of people, and I am proud to say that in those years, only one complaint was made against me, the one by the Attorney-General then, Mr Tan Boon Teik. I believe that that complaint was politically motivated because I was defending JB Jeyaretnam.

I have also been betrayed by some whom I consider friends. I have taken those betrayals in my stride although they hurt initially, but I survived them. I do not know how true it is when they say that they are praying for me and for me to live a long time. Most are definitely genuine and true to heart. How many lawyers can boast of such loyalty and support from friends?

My wife would tell me, "I hear my friends say that you are different, you know? Despite all the publicity, you have not forgotten your humility. You never fail to greet those who greet you even if they are strangers. People appreciate that. Don't underestimate yourself." Diana will say, "You are a different sort of lawyer. Your looks mislead because you are, in fact, one of the kindest people I know. It is because of your kindness and your compassion that I was inspired to become a criminal lawyer. I don't think anybody could be what you are. I will try and make sure that we don't let the principles that you inculcated in us disappear."

I read the last page of my first book where I said at the end, "Years have passed and I really appreciate that at least some people recognise some of the good things I have done. I have in my twilight years become some sort of celebrity but I wonder how long that will last. People have short memories and very easily you can become yesterday's hero."

It has been six years now since I wrote my first book and there is still interest in it. I like to think that I am not yesterday's hero as people still remember me and as long as some still remember my work, I will be happy. I don't think I will be writing a third book for my health is deteriorating and I find it so hard to concentrate.

A TRIBUTE TO SUBHAS ANANDAN

THE FOLLOWING TRIBUTES WERE FIRST PUBLISHED IN *AL-MIZAN*, **A PUBLICATION OF THE ASSOCIATION OF MUSLIM LAWYERS, IN CONNECTION WITH "THE YELLOW RIBBON SUBHAS ANANDAN STAR BURSARY AWARD". THIS EDUCATION FUND FOR EX-INMATES WAS LAUNCHED ON 28 OCTOBER 2014 AT THE SUPREME COURT.**

"The Singapore Criminal Bar, unlike criminal bars of some Commonwealth jurisdictions, has not been fortunate to produce many well-regarded legendary criminal practitioners. In recent memory the most notable was the late David Saul Marshall.

Subhas is a man of integrity, boundless energy, passion, compassion, generosity and a staunch defender of the Rule of Law. All these called for hard work and commitment which Subhas wholeheartedly gave. When David Marshall ceased practice in 1978, Subhas Anandan was in his 7th year of practice. As you all may recollect, Subhas was notorious then. But in the 43 years of legal practice, he has developed himself into an outstanding criminal lawyer we have today at the Singapore Criminal Bar."

Rajan Menon
Senior Partner, RHTLaww Taylor Wessing LLP

"I congratulate Subhas on more than four illustrious decades in the law. I had the pleasure of working closely with him and several other senior members of the Criminal Bar during my stint as the Attorney-General. Subhas was always helpful and constructive. I am pleased that his colleagues have chosen to honour him in this way and extend my best wishes to him on this happy occasion."

The Honourable Chief Justice Sundaresh Menon

"Subhas' passionate dedication to help his clients, his inimitable style, wit and personality, has made him a giant of the Criminal Bar. Subhas' cases are legendary. So I am glad that members of the Bar are paying tribute to him through this Journal. And it is a tribute to him that he has continued to fight for the underprivileged in the Courts pro bono, only a few months after being hospitalized. All of us wish Subhas good health."

K Shanmugam
Minister for Law and Foreign Affairs

"I see Subhas as a man who, beyond his grizzly growl, quietly strives to live life with spiritual purpose and meaning, faithful to his beliefs and convictions. He believes in the need to balance the odds for the underdog, because it is the fair thing to do, the right thing to do. And he just goes ahead and does it, year after year — no pontification, just action. And by his so doing, case by case, regardless of individual outcome, his compassion touches the lives of so many, in so many ways, for the better."

Benny Lim
Permanent Secretary, Prime Minister's Office
and long-time friend of Subhas

"Mr Subhas Anandan or "Subhas" as he is affectionately known to members of the legal community, has, as a lawyer, made a meaningful difference to the legal landscape, and in particular, to the administration of criminal justice.

For almost four decades, he has taken on a number of the most problematic criminal cases and represented a number of disagreeable individuals. Despite this, he has achieved some notable legal successes. Not a few of his cases have become landmarks in the legal landscape. Subhas is well respected by Bench and Bar for his admirable forthrightness in the presentation of his legal submissions and an uncanny legal acumen that can identify the most persuasive points to be made even in apparently "hopeless" cases.

He has been a pioneer in promoting pro bono services long before this gained recognition as constituting an essential facet of legal practice. In establishing the Association of Criminal Lawyers, Subhas has given the Criminal Bar a distinctive voice that is not just heard but one that has also often influenced policy making. His remarkable resilience, extraordinary fortitude and boundless optimism in overcoming many professional and personal challenges bear further mention. All in all, he is a lawyer with a good head, a big heart and an "uncommon' touch". The legal community is indebted to Subhas for his many noteworthy contributions."

VK Rajah, SC
Attorney-General of Singapore

"It really is a pleasure having to say something concerning Subhas. It would be difficult if not well-nigh impossible to write a short note on Subhas. His care and concern for his clients is exemplary and sterling. His attitude and concern became a hallmark in rendering service to his clients. It is quite frankly a hard act to follow. Subhas pays very little heed to fees. His openness and frank remarks became legendary. Subhas is justly and fondly regarded as the Father of the Association of Criminal Lawyers in Singapore. This is regarded as one of Singapore's pro bono legal organisations. The fact that ACLS is recognised as a true and respected participant of the legal profession in Singapore is due to a large measure the role Subhas has played."

Harry Elias, SC
Founder and Consultant, Harry Elias Partnership

"I am privileged to have been asked to add a few words to the tributes which Subhas richly deserves. I have had the honour of knowing him since his admission to the Bar, and to have been a neighbor of this extraordinary man for some 14 years. His courage as an advocate, combined with his knowledge of criminal law and procedure, stand him out as a leading practitioner of that branch of the profession. I should add that, when required, he affects a fearsome demenour which only adds to his persuasiveness. These qualities he readily makes available gratis, to those who cannot afford his fees.

Subhas has not been in the best of health recently, but as his friends and colleagues fully expected, he has battled through his problems, and it is a pleasure and a relief to see him, surrounded by colleagues, pupils and diverse admirers, holding forth at the Singapore Cricket Club during lunch adjournments, ready to battle on when hearings resume."

Joseph Grimberg, SC
Consultant, Drew & Napier LLC

"I have known Subhas for many years. He is an honourable and distinguished member of our legal profession. He always tries to present the best possible case for his clients. He is kind and helpful. Let me share with you an incident which showed Subhas' generosity and pro bono work.

In 2002 Subhas represented Lam Chen Fong, a remittance agent who was faced with more than 1,000 charges of criminal breach of trust. The money belonged to more than 1,000 Chinese workers. It was their hard-earned money. A total of the $9 million of the Chinese workers' salaries did not reach their loved ones in China. The Commercial Affairs Department (CAD) could only recover about 10 per cent of the money despite its best efforts. Understandably, the victims were very emotional and distressed over their losses. I was then the Director of CAD and I informed Subhas that the accused had paid his legal fee from the fruit of his crime. I told him of the plight of the victims and that it would go a long way if he could donate his legal fee to the victims. Subhas graciously agreed and a cheque of $20,000 was given to the victims. He continued to represent his client on a pro bono basis. He is indeed a man with a big heart and has done the legal profession proud."

Justice Tan Siong Thye

"Subhas and I were colleagues in my early years of practice. Subhas taught me that criminal practice is about compassion and helping others. Beneath that outward gangsta appearance is a man known for his humour, generosity and heart of gold. He is a friend in need, a friend indeed."

Tan Chee Meng, SC
Deputy Managing Partner, Wong Partnership

"Subhas is a legend in the legal fraternity. While he is respected for his integrity, sense of fair play and professionalism, it is his heartfelt compassion for and devotion to the cause of the downtrodden that have made him a giant among lawyers. His is a remarkable story of a man whose courage and convictions have become the stuff of folklore. Subhas has always endeavoured to use the law to serve the cause of righteousness. He has taken so many firm steps in that noble and admirable journey that the huge and enduring footprints that they formed will never be filled by anyone else."

Davinder Singh, SC
CEO, Drew & Napier

"Subhas is a very special lawyer and friend. His immense contribution to the Criminal Bar in Singapore is unparelled. I once asked Subhas why he chose to defend someone accused of a particularly serious offence and pro bono to boot. He replied, "My client is innocent and even if he is found guilty, he probably made a mistake and everyone makes mistakes. But that is no reason why he should not get the best defence possible." I believe that this shows the true measure of Subhas."

Michael Palmer
Director, Quahe Woo & Palmer LLC

SPEECH BY SUBHAS ANANDAN ON THE OCCASION OF "A TRIBUTE TO
SUBHAS ANANDAN", ORGANISED BY THE ASSOCIATION OF MUSLIM
LAWYERS, 28 OCTOBER 2014, AT THE SUPREME COURT.

The Honourable Mr SR Nathan, The Honourable Minister for
Foreign Affairs & Law, The Honourable AG, Justices of Appeal,
Judges and Judicial Commissioners, Supreme Court, District Judges,
distinguished guests and friends.

I thank the Muslim Lawyers Association for organising this tribute
to me and it is even more prestigious for me because it's a Muslim
organisation that is honouring a non-Muslim, and I think this happens
maybe only in Singapore. That shows our religious harmony. I thank
the Minister, Mr Shanmugam, for visiting me in the hospital and at
home and to tell me that I should not resign from the committees
that he has appointed me to because he was confident I would recover
and be back on my feet. He told me that one of the first things I can
do is to go to the temple where I'm the Chairman of the Board of
Trustees to pray. And I said, "OK". Today I think on hindsight prayers,
not only mine but everybody else's prayers, have been answered in a
limited way because I still have to go for retreatment.

I must thank Court of Appeal Justices Chao Hick Tin and Andrew
Phang. When I appeared before them on a pro bono case, the first
thing Justice of Appeal Chao said was, "Mr Anandan, it's good to see
you back in court." And Justice of Appeal Andrew Phang told me,
"You don't have to stand up, you can sit down and conduct the case."
I declined the offer because I can't imagine appearing in the highest
tribunal sitting down. But this shows the compassion of these two

judges. I thank you for that. I'm really touched.

I went for a lunch organised by the Muslim Lawyers Association. I saw Mr VK Rajah, who came to talk to me. He was just made AG and he told me, "You're looking better and you got my email. You can always send me an email and I will create the time for you to have thosai lunch with you." And that offer coming from a man ... is so special. I was really privileged, was very happy. I've not taken up the offer yet but I can tell you I will.

I went to the Subordinate Courts. I saw the presiding judge. Mr See Kee Oon came out to welcome me and said it was good to see me. He said all the judicial officers of the state courts know your condition. If you are tired, you just have to tell them and there will be a break. And when I appeared before District Judge Shaiffudin to conduct a case, he told me in chambers as well as in open court, "If you're tired, Mr Anandan, just sit. We will adjourn the cases on dialysis days, that is on Mondays, Wednesdays and Fridays. If you inform us early, we will do that." I was very touched by the way the Judicial Officers treated me. The compassion they have shown and I said to myself, "The accused persons will be very lucky because it seems that there is a change in the judicial temperament. It seems to be more compassionate." I was in the sub courts, I saw young DPPs coming towards me saying, "Mr Anandan, it's good to see you." When I went to the AG's Chambers for a meeting, the senior DPPs came to see how I was. One young DPP whom I did not know came to talk to me. I was very proud of the fact that at least today we don't behave as though we are enemies. At least there is friendly attitude and I think the new AG can enhance this relationship even better and I hope he does.

Now there are others I would like to thank. I can't name everybody. But I must thank my fellow senior partner, Rajan Menon, for visiting me quite frequently in the hospital and in my home. When I told him I wanted to retire as a senior partner, he said, "No. You don't decide when you retire. We will decide when you should retire. And when we say that, you do that. You just get well." I'm grateful to him for that.

Then I'm grateful to my nephew, Sunil Sudheesan, who is a junior partner of the firm, and Diana Ngiam – they said she is the daughter I did not have and I thank God I did not have her [laughter]. They took my department through stormy weather and held the ship steadfastly and they are still holding the fort. They are my left and right hands and without them, I'm not actually much.

I must thank Lawrence Quahe, Chris Woo, Michael Palmer, Chentil and the partners of Quahe, Woo & Palmer for visiting me often in the hospital and coming to my home with lunch and telling me, "You should not worry because whatever happens, there will always be a space for you and your team in our place. So do not ever worry about the future. We will always be there to take care." I said I am in an enviable position as my firm has not asked me to retire yet. So you have to put it on hold but I thanked them for the friendship they have shown me.

I must thank two other people, Bajwa and my old friend Angela Lee. Both of them would come and sit beside me whenever they can when I am undergoing dialysis. It is a very depressing procedure. They tried to cheer me up. I thank them.

And Joe Grimberg, my neighbour, visited me in hospital, came to the house many times. He is on the 13th floor and I am on the 10th. Visiting my house was not a big deal. But he came and told my wife, took her one side and said, "I am a rich old Jewish man," as though we didn't know he is a man. "I got a lot of money, why don't you give me all the medical bills and I can settle it." The bills were quite high but my wife said, "No, it's okay. We can manage." "Promise me one thing, if you ever want any money, just tell me." And while I was in hospital, he gave Edward D'Souza a blank cheque saying if whenever I needed the money to draw on it. I'm really grateful to Joe

With Joe at our condo garden.

Grimberg for that kind gesture. Mr Edward D'Souza, who is a bachelor, shrinking away as you can see. He rang up my wife to say, "You know, I am a bachelor. I got a small flat and I don't need much money. All that is yours to give Subhas the best treatment." I thank you also Eddie for your generous offer. Both of you don't think you have escaped. I may call upon you.

Now, finally, to talk about my family. Right now I have three siblings. My eldest, Dr Subhashini, she is not only my personal physician but personal physician for all my siblings. And I am not exaggerating when I say my sister, my Chechy, as I said has saved my life a number of times — by being there, staying with me in hospital and looking after me.

My brother, Sudheesan, gave me the confidence and courage that otherwise I will not have because I know he is there. Silently strong, and you know he is so dependable. Never lets you down.

My younger sister, Sugadha. She was my spiritual supporter. She does all the religious things necessary for my well-being. Spends hours with me in my house listening to *bajans* and music. I owe her a great deal too.

My late brother, Surash, who died 14 years ago, trying to save passengers from a burning plane, was my greatest fan. I still miss him a lot. He contributed to what I am. My siblings and my parents together made me what I am today. They moulded my character. So if I have done anything bad, blame them, not me.

And then my son, Sujesh, who is studying law in Nottingham University; that will make the late judge, Punch Coomaraswamy, a happy man because he swears by Nottingham University. He was not only a mentor but also a good friend.

Surash with nephews Sunil and Sujesh, and niece Sunita.

And finally, I would like to thank my wife. She is not only my wife, she is my best friend and there were many occasions when I had to literally lean on her shoulder because I couldn't walk. Thank you for having wide shoulders. Many a time, I have shed tears of frustration and despair on her shoulders. I must thank her for one thing — she and my elder sister defied the doctor's orders and did not take me back home to die as some people would say. They will keep me in hospital and do their best. Prayers will help. I am glad they defied the doctor's orders for if not, most probably, I won't be here standing talking to you.

And today has been a very happy day for me. A wonderful day in a sense that I'm surrounded by people whom I respect and people whom I love. I am so happy that if I don't have any tomorrows, it doesn't matter because I have today to remember.

The Yellow Ribbon Subhas Anandan Star Bursary Award event was held on 28 October 2014, at the Supreme Court Auditorium. The Guest-of-Honour was Mr K Shanmugam.

Above, from left: Philip Tan, Chairman of the Yellow Ribbon Fund, Noor Marican, K Shanmugam and Subhas.

Left, top: With dear friends, Tan Hee Teck and his wife Sally. Left, bottom: With old friend chef Violet Oon and former Singapore President SR Nathan.

THESE PAGES: CONDOLENCE MESSAGES FROM STUDENTS OF PIONEER JUNIOR COLLEGE ON THE PASSING OF SUBHAS ANANDAN ON 7 JANUARY 2015.

Our thoughts & prayers are with the family in this difficult time.

Mr Anandan's selfless generosity has inspired our Pioneers through his gift of the GP Book Prize. His legacy will live on.

With deepest sympathy,
PJC English Department

you're truly an inspiration. I really hope that one day, I will be able to do the same as you

You will always remain in our ♡'s & minds
PJC 14A04.

— Deepest Condolences. Your legacy lives on forever. Thank you, & goodbye
—PJC 14S

For An Extraordinary Man who touched Ordinary lives. You'll be sorely missed
Mr Laleena (L7/GP)

I respect you for being the man you are

In life, a beacon of hope.
In death, a light of inspiration.
Mr Anandan, you will be remembered.

Thank you for your selfless contribution to justice. You will be dearly missed.
May your legacy live on. Rest in peace.
- On behalf of 14S09 PJC

Deepest condolences to the family and I believe he was a great man and will be remembered in Singapore for being simply great :)

Thank you for giving a second chance to the people who needed it most; and a WONDERFUL inspiration for this generation -

- from 15th Student Council

"If only there was enough space on this tiny card to evoke my unfettered joie de vivre for what you have done! You'll be greatly remembered. ♥"